The

Physical Education Teacher's

The
Physical Education Teacher's

Marian D. Milliken, M.Ed.

Parker Publishing Company
Paramus, NJ 07652

Library of Congress Cataloging-in-Publication Data

Milliken, Marian D.
    The physical education teacher's book of lists / Marian D. Milliken.
        p. cm.
    ISBN 0-13-021334-9
    1. Physical education and training—Handouts, manuals, etc.   2. Sports—Handbooks,
manuals, etc.   I. Title: Book of lists.   II. Title.
    GV341 .M665 2001
    613.7—dc21   2001021963

Acquisitions Editor: Connie Kallback
Production Editor: Jacqueline Roulette
Interior Formatting: Inkwell Publishing Services
Art Formatter: Christy McCall

Printed in the United States of America

10 9 8 7 6 5 4 3

ISBN   0-13-021334-9

ATTENTION: CORPORATIONS AND SCHOOLS
Parker books are available at quantity discounts with bulk purchase for educational,
business, or sales promotional use. For information, please write to: Prentice Hall
Special Sales, 240 Frisch Court, Paramus, NJ 07652. Please supply: title of book, ISBN,
quantity, how the book will be used, date needed.

PARKER PUBLISHING COMPANY
Paramus, NJ 07652

www.phedu.com

DEDICATION

This book is dedicated to the three people who make up
my most favorite list of them all,

The joys of my life—My Children

Lisa R. Milliken
Christine D. McCall
Troy E. Milliken

ACKNOWLEDGMENTS

The clip art used throughout this book was acquired from Nova Development Corporation's Gold Edition ART EXPLOSION 600,000 Images 1995–1998, which has proven to be an invaluable tool for desktop publishing. Further information about this software can be obtained by accessing http://www.novadevcorp.com.

Very special thanks to:

My daughter, Christy McCall, for endless hours of research and design patiently offered with enthusiasm, laughter, and love. Your smile can light up the world.

Robert Michael Ziemba, for joyous laughter, quiet patience, and gentle strength. You have filled my heart and touched my soul.

My family, for providing me with never-ending encouragement, support, laughter, and love. I am indeed blessed to have you all in my life.

My editor, Connie Kallback, for generous guidance and insight patiently offered with humor and understanding.

My friends, for providing support and encouragement.

And my students, all of you, for everything you have taught me.

ABOUT THE AUTHOR

Marian D. Milliken, M.Ed., has taught Health and Physical Education for over 20 years in the Council Rock School District in Newtown, PA, and has coached field hockey, softball, track, and gymnastics. During her professional career, Marian has served as Recreational Coordinator for Northampton Township, Bucks County, PA, and has also served her community by serving on the Northampton Township Parks and Recreation Board. She is co-author with Patricia Rizzo-Toner of the *Health Teacher's Book of Lists* (The Center for Applied Research in Education, 1999).

Besides her work as a teacher and coach, Marian is also the proud advisor to the Newtown Junior High School S.A.D.D. (Students Against Doing Drugs) program, which, since initiating in 1993, has grown to over 1,200 members. She has further promoted wellness and physical fitness awareness by coordinating the Junior High School D.A.R.E. program with the local police department and by developing a highly successful walking/jogging program available to all students and staff. A member of AAHPERD, NASPE, and NAGWS, Marian received the prestigious Hammond Service Award from Trenton State College in NJ, and has been recognized by the Pennsylvania Commission on Crime and Delinquency, and the Northampton Township Board of Supervisors for her achievements. She has honored herself and her school district by being nominated for Disney's American Teacher Awards and being named to *Who's Who in American Education*.

ABOUT THIS RESOURCE

For Physical Education teachers, both beginning and established, in grades K–12, here is a comprehensive resource, including over 200 informative lists you can reproduce for student use or keep on hand as a reference in planning sports, games, and activities.

The *Physical Education Teacher's Book of Lists* is an easy-to-use resource for the busy educator, including goals and objectives, Adapted Physical Education considerations, historical facts, basic rules of the games, field and playing area dimensions, equipment needs, safety hints, metric conversions, tournaments, and national associations and organizations including websites.

For ease of use, these lists have been organized into three sections.

➡ **Section 1: Goals** provides lists illustrating the purpose of Physical Education in schools, containing the aim, objectives, and outcomes of the program including the "Stages of Human Development," "Physical Education Career Ideas," and "Modification of Activities for Adapted Physical Education."

> You've got a goal,
> I've got a goal,
> Now all we need is a football team.
> —*Groucho Marx*

➡ **Section 2: Games** is an alphabetical listing of over 35 sports and activities, each of which includes lists such as "Field, Court, or Playing Area Diagrams," "Equipment," "Players and Positions," "Basic Rules of the Game," "Terminology," "Safety Hints," "Etiquette," and "Historical Facts."

> If I hear it, I forget.
> If I see it, I remember.
> If I do it, I learn.
> —*Chinese Proverb*

➥ **Section 3: Guides** offers supplementary lists of information vital to the development of a successful Physical Education program, including "Metric and United States Distance Equivalents," "Metric Conversion Charts," "Olympic Facts," "Fitness Tests," "Tournament Guides," "Ways to Praise," and "National Associations and Organizations."

> I keep six honest serving men
> (They taught me all I know)
> Their names are What and Where and When,
> And How and Why and Who.
>
> —*Rudyard Kipling*

I hope you'll find these collected lists useful in your daily Physical Education planning and instruction.

Marian D. Milliken

CONTENTS

SECTION 1

GOALS

SECTION 2

GAMES

SECTION 3

GUIDES

Goals

1. DEFINITION OF A PHYSICALLY EDUCATED PERSON

The National Association for Sport and Physical Education (NASPE) developed the definition of a physically educated person in 1990. A physically educated person:

➡ Has skills necessary to perform a variety of physical activities.

➡ Is physically fit.

➡ Participates regularly in physical activity.

➡ Knows the implications of and the benefits from involvement in physical activities.

➡ Values physical activity and its contribution to a healthful lifestyle.

2. OBJECTIVES OF PHYSICAL EDUCATION

Physical education is unique in that it has the potential to contribute to the education and development of the entire individual through the medium of movement.

Psychomotor Objectives

➡ Physical fitness, which includes nutrition, health habits, exercise, and the development of body control and coordination.

Cognitive Objectives

➡ The accumulation of knowledge, and the ability to think, evaluate, make judgments, and interpret that knowledge.

Affective Objectives

➡ The development of traits such as the individual's values, attitudes, ideals, and interests.

3. CONTENT STANDARDS IN PHYSICAL EDUCATION

Content standards simply specify what a student should know and be able to do. In physical education this involves not only the knowledge but also the skills that a student is expected to learn.

According to the National Association for Sport and Physical Education, a physically educated person:

➡ Demonstrates competency in many movement forms and proficiency in a few movement forms.

➡ Applies movement concepts and principles to the learning and development of motor skills.

➡ Exhibits a physically active lifestyle.

➡ Achieves and maintains a health-enhancing level of physical fitness.

➡ Demonstrates responsible personal and social behavior in physical activity settings.

➡ Demonstrates understanding and respect for differences among people in physical activity settings.

➡ Understands that physical activity provides opportunities for enjoyment, challenge, self-expression, and social interaction.

For more information, see *Moving into the Future, National Physical Education Standards: A Guide to Content and Assessment.* Developed by the National Association for Sport and Physical Education, WCB McGraw-Hill, 1995.

4. SKILLS DESIRED BY *FORTUNE* 500 COMPANIES

In 1990 the *Creative Education Foundation* listed the following skills desired by *Fortune* 500 companies in order of importance:

➡ Teamwork

➡ Problem Solving

➡ Interpersonal Skills

➡ Oral Communication

➡ Listening

➡ Personal/Career Development

➡ Creative Thinking

➡ Leadership

➡ Goal setting/Motivation

➡ Writing

➡ Organizational Effectiveness

➡ Computation

➡ Reading

5. BASIC PHYSICAL EDUCATION PROGRAM CONTENT

Federal legislation mandates that physical education programs be equally available to both genders (Title IX) as well as to disabled students (Individuals with Disabilities Education Act).

Elementary-Level Programs

→ Large muscle, locomotor skills:

- Walking
- Running
- Skipping
- Jumping
- Hopping
- Galloping
- Leaping

→ Large muscle, nonlocomotor skills:

- Bending
- Twisting
- Turning
- Lowering
- Reaching
- Lifting
- Raising

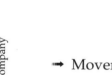

→ Movement skills:

- Flexibility
- Balance
- Agility
- Spatial Awareness

→ Basic elements of physical activities such as:

- Soccer
- Volleyball
- Fitness
- Basketball
- Baseball
- Dance

Middle-Level Programs

→ More advanced skill development with a broader range of activities and an emphasis on team sports to encourage the development of social skills.

Senior High School Programs

→ Designed to help students gain an understanding of the personal and social effects of physical exercise and wellness.

→ Continued participation in competitive activities and lifetime sports encourages continued interpersonal skill development.

6. MASLOW'S HIERARCHY OF NEEDS

American psychologist Abraham Maslow developed a ranked order of needs that human beings must have to survive and grow. The most basic physical needs, such as hunger and thirst, must be satisfied before a human being becomes aware of and is able to meet additional emotional needs, such as love and recognition.

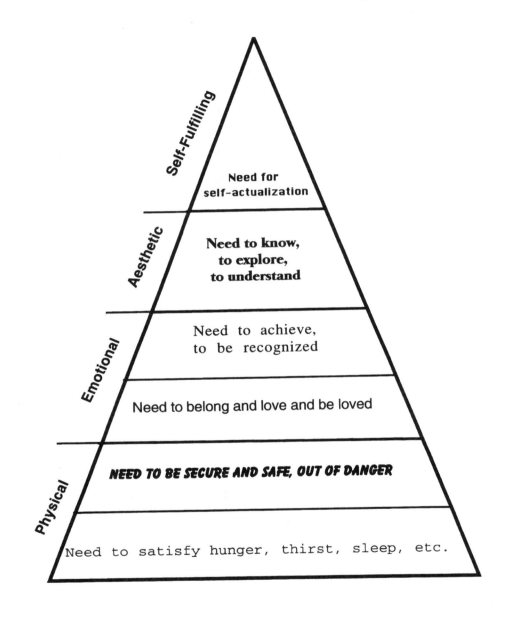

7. HUMAN BODY TYPES

In 1940, W. H. Sheldon used the three primary layers of the embryonic germ cell layers (endoderm, mesoderm, and ectoderm) to describe the differences in body build.

➡ *Endomorph:*   Dominant viscera with roundness and softness.

➡ *Mesomorph:*   Solid and firm with excellent musculature, prominent bones, and heavy underlying tissues.

➡ *Ectomorph:*   Linear, fragile, and delicate body with slender bones, thin muscles, and greater surface area in proportion to mass.

8. STAGES OF HUMAN DEVELOPMENT

Erik Erikson describes eight stages of human development in his theory of psychosocial development. Two of these stages span the public school years.

Stage	Ages	Basic Conflict	Important Event	Summary
Oral–Sensory	Birth to 12–18 months	Trust/Mistrust	Feeding	The infant must have a first loving, trusting relationship with the caregiver or risk developing a sense of mistrust.
Muscular-Anal	18 months–3 years	Autonomy/ Shame and/or Doubt	Toilet training	The child's energies go toward developing physical skills, such as walking, grasping, and rectal sphincter control. He or she learns control but may develop shame and doubt if the training period is not handled well.
Locomotor	3–6 years	Initiative/ Guilt	Independence	The child takes more initiative and becomes more assertive but may be too forceful, which may lead to guilt feelings.
Latency	6–12 years	Industry/ Inferiority	School	The child must respond to learning new skills or possibly risk feeling inferior, incompetent, or have a general sense of failure.
Adolescence	12–18 years	Identity/ Role Confusion	Peer relationships	The teenager must gain a sense of identity in sex roles, politics, work, and spirituality.
Young Adulthood	19 to 40 years	Intimacy/ Isolation	Love relationships	The young adult must develop intimate relationships or suffer feelings of isolation.
Middle Adulthood	40–65 years	Generatively/ Stagnation	Parenting	Each adult must find a way to help and support the next generation.
Maturity	65–death	Ego Integrity/ Despair	Reflection on and acceptance of one's life	Knowing who you are and feeling fulfilled is the final stage of human development.

© 2001 Parker Publishing Company

For more information, see Erikson, E. H.: *Childhood and Society*, Second Edition, New York: W. W. Norton, & Co., 1963.

9. PHYSICAL EDUCATION CAREER OPPORTUNITIES

Areas of Specialization

→ Exercise Physiology

→ Motor Development

→ Biomechanics

→ Sport History

→ Sport Psychology

→ Sport Sociology

→ Measurement and Evaluation

Professional Applications

→ Sports Medicine

→ Athletic Training

→ Sports Journalism

→ Fitness Management

→ Cardiac Rehabilitation

→ Sports Management/Business

→ Sports Photography

→ Physical Therapy

→ Exercise Testing

→ Facility Design

→ Robotics

→ Teaching

10. FEDERAL STATUTES PROHIBITING DISCRIMINATION IN EDUCATION

The U.S. Department of Education's Office for Civil Rights (OCR) enforces five federal statutes that prohibit discrimination in education programs and activities that receive federal financial assistance:

→ *Title VI of the Civil Rights Act of 1964*, which prohibits discrimination on the basis of race, color, and national origin, is prohibited;

→ *Title IX of the Education Amendments of 1972*, which prohibits sex discrimination;

→ *Section 504 of the Rehabilitation Act of 1973*, which prohibits discrimination on the basis of disability;

→ *The Age Discrimination Act of 1975*, which prohibits age discrimination; and

→ *Title II of the Americans with Disabilities Act of 1990*.

OCR consists of administrative offices that are located at the U.S. Department of Education's national headquarters in Washington, D.C., and 12 enforcement offices around the country.

11. LAWS PERTAINING TO ADAPTED PHYSICAL EDUCATION

➡ The *Individuals with Disabilities Education Act (IDEA),* originally Public Law 94-142, requires schools to develop, according to specific standards, an individualized education program (IEP) for each eligible student with disabilities. An IEP that meets the requirements of the IDEA also fulfills the requirements of Section 504 and Title II of the ADA. An appropriate education for a disabled student is designed to ensure the following rights for students with disabilities:

- Right to a free, appropriate education
- Right to nondiscriminatory testing, evaluation, and placement procedures
- Right to be educated in the least restrictive environment
- Right to procedural due process of law

➡ *Section 504 of the Rehabilitation Act of 1973* essentially declared that individuals with disabilities could not be excluded from any program or activity receiving federal funds, based solely on the disability. In physical education and in intramural, extracurricular, or interscholastic athletics, a reasonable accommodation must be made to include a student with disabilities who wishes to participate.

➡ *Title II of the Americans with Disabilities Act, 1990* prohibits discrimination on the basis of disability by state and local governments in employment, public accommodations, transportation, state and local government services, and telecommunication relay services. The primary impact on Adapted Physical Education is its implications as it relates to recreation and sport facilities such as golf courses, bowling alleys, ski centers, canoe rental sites, etc.

12. DISABILITIES COVERED UNDER SECTION 504 OF THE REHABILITATION ACT OF 1973

The Section 504 regulation defines an "individual with handicaps" as any person who:

➡ Has a physical or mental impairment that substantially limits one or more major life activities

➡ Has a record of such impairment

➡ Is regarded as having such impairment

The regulation further defines a physical or mental impairment as:

➡ (A) any physiological disorder or condition, cosmetic disfigurement, or anatomical loss affecting one or more of the following body systems: neurological; musculoskeletal; special sense organs; respiratory, including speech organs; cardiovascular; reproductive; digestive; genitourinary; hemic and lymphatic; skin; and endocrine

➡ (B) any mental or psychological disorder, such as mental retardation, organic brain syndrome, emotional or mental illness, and specific learning disabilities

13. OBJECTIVES OF ADAPTED PHYSICAL EDUCATION

➠ To help students to improve those conditions that can be improved

➠ To help students protect themselves and any conditions that could be aggravated through certain physical activities

➠ To provide students with an opportunity to learn and to participate in a number of appropriate recreational and lifetime sports and activities

➠ To improve physical fitness through the maximal development of organic and neuro-muscular systems

➠ To help each student develop a knowledge and appreciation of his or her physical and mental limitations

➠ To help students make social adjustments and develop a feeling of self worth and value

➠ To aid each student in developing knowledge and appreciation relative to good body mechanics

➠ To help students understand and appreciate a variety of sports they can enjoy as nonparticipants or spectators

14. MODIFICATION OF ACTIVITIES FOR ADAPTED PHYSICAL EDUCATION

Through the use of minor modifications, almost any physical education activity can be made safe and interesting for students in the Adapted Physical Education program. Rules, techniques, and equipment for an activity should be changed as little as possible when being modified for the Adapted Physical Education student. Some ways to modify a Physical Education program include the following:

➡ The size of the playing area can be made smaller, reducing the amount of required physical activity.

➡ Larger pieces of equipment can be introduced to make the game easier or to slow down the pace of the activity.

➡ Smaller, lighter pieces of equipment or an object that is easier to handle may be used.

➡ Additional players can be added to a team, reducing the amount of activity and the amount of responsibility required from each player.

➡ Minor rule changes can be made while retaining as many of the basic rules as possible.

➡ Total amount of time for the activity can be reduced.

➡ Players can be required to rotate positions frequently in order for all participants to have the opportunity to perform various kinds of activities and play different positions.

➡ The number of points required to win a contest can be reduced.

➡ Free substitutions can be made, allowing participants the opportunity to have sufficient rest periods while the activity continues.

Games

Match Point	Point that, if won by the server, wins the match for that server.
Midcourt	Middle third of the court.
Receiver	Player to whom the shuttle is served.
Server	Player who puts the shuttle into play.
Setting	Choosing the number of points to play when certain tie scores are reached.
Shuttlecock (Shuttle)	Feathered plastic or nylon object that is volleyed back and forth over the net.
Side Out	When the serve is lost.
Smash	Fast, downward overhead stroke.
Underhand	Stroke that is hit upward from below shoulder level.

30. HISTORICAL FACTS ABOUT BASEBALL

➡ Traced back to a game called *stoolball*, which was played during the Middle Ages in England.

➡ A batter attempted to hit a pitched ball before it reached a stool. The batter ran around three stools and back to the "homestool" if the ball was hit.

➡ In the seventeenth century, British children played *rounders*, which was closely related to baseball except that the fielders threw the ball at the runner to get the out.

➡ The colonists brought rounders to America in the early 1700s.

➡ Baseball was referred to in an eighteenth-century book published in England and printed in America.

➡ Historians report that Abner Doubleday, a West Point Cadet, invented the game at Cooperstown, New York in 1839.

➡ Alexander Cartwright, a surveyor, is credited with developing standard rules in 1845.

➡ The first game was played under the new rules in June 1846.

➡ Games were being played for nine innings by 1858 and there was an association of amateur players.

➡ During the Civil War, soldiers from the east taught the game to others from all parts of the country.

➡ The 1869 Cincinnati Red Stockings was the first all-professional team.

➡ An association of professional players was formed in 1871.

➡ Pitching was underhand and no gloves were worn during this time.

➡ The National League was formed in 1876 and the American League began in 1900.

➡ American missionaries introduced the game to Japan in the 1870s.

➡ Baseball became an Olympic sport in 1992.

© 2001 Parker Publishing Company

31. BASEBALL EQUIPMENT

Bat   Smooth cylinder made of wood, aluminum, magnesium, or graphite-composite, the maximum diameter of which is 2 3/4 inches and maximum length of which is 36 inches or less. The handle may be covered with material up to 18 inches to improve the batter's grip. A bat may not weigh, numerically, more than five ounces less than the length of the bat.

Ball   A sphere formed by yarn wound around a small core of cork, rubber, or similar material covered with two strips of white horsehide or cowhide. It is 9 to 9 1/4 inches in circumference and weighs 5 to 5 1/4 ounces.

Gloves   Gloves are made of leather. Fielders' gloves have four fingers connected to the thumb by a web and have a maximum height of 14 inches and a maximum width of 8 inches. The first baseman's glove, or mitt, is padded with no fingers. The catcher's mitt does not have to conform to these specifications.

Shoes   Baseball shoes may not have pointed spikes.

Protective   Batters must wear helmets with earflaps and catchers must wear head, throat and body protection, and knee and shin guards.

Home plate   Five-sided white rubber base that sits flush to the ground. It measures 17 inches wide across the edge facing the pitcher, 8 1/2 inches long on each side, and 12 inches long on the sides of the point facing the catcher.

Bases   White 15-inch square bags made of canvas, rubber, or synthetic material.

Pitcher's Plate White 6 by 24-inch rectangular rubber slab.

32. BASEBALL FIELD

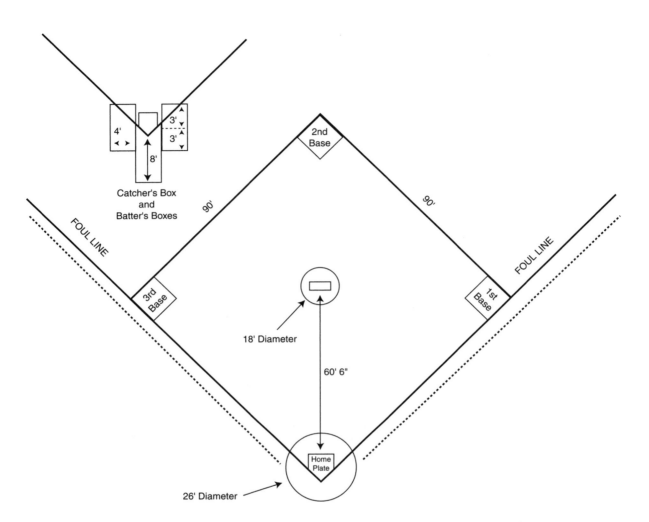

4'

3'

3'

8'

Catcher's Box
and
Batter's Boxes

2nd
Base

90'

90'

FOUL LINE

FOUL LINE

3rd
Base

1st
Base

18' Diameter

60' 6"

Home
Plate

26' Diameter

33. BASEBALL POSITIONS

With the exception of the pitcher and catcher, fielders may stand anywhere in fair playing territory. The pitcher must start in fair territory on the pitching plate and the catcher must start in foul territory in the catcher's box.

Players bat in the order listed.

➡ The Battery

       1-Pitcher

       2-Catcher

➡ Infielders

       3-First Base

       4-Second Base

       5-Third Base

       6-Shortstop

➡ Outfielders

       7-Left Field

       8-Center Field

       9-Right Field

➡ Designated Hitter: In some games, a DH may be named before the game to bat in place of the pitcher. The DH has a permanent position in the batting order and may not play defense. If the DH is put in as a fielder, there may no longer be a DH and the pitcher must bat in the place of the fielder who was replaced by the DH. The DH may be replaced by a pinch hitter who takes his or her place in the batting order. A replaced DH may not come back into the game.

34. BASIC RULES OF BASEBALL

➡ The game is divided into nine innings.

➡ During each inning, each team takes a turn to play offense by taking its turn at bat and to play defense in the field.

➡ The bottom half of the ninth inning does not have to be played and the inning is considered complete if the home team (who always bats last) is ahead.

➡ If the game is tied, extra innings are played until one team has more runs at the end of a complete inning.

➡ A game stopped due to rain, darkness, etc., will be counted as a complete game if five complete innings have been played.

➡ The *home team* is the team on whose field the game is being played.

➡ An *out* occurs when batters or base runners are prevented from safely reaching or advancing to a base.

➡ The batting team is allowed three outs each inning.

➡ When a batting team has acquired three outs, it retires to the field to play defense and the team that was in the field takes a turn at bat.

➡ A run is scored for the batting team each time a base runner successfully reaches first base, second base, third base, and home plate before the third out of an inning.

35. BASIC BASEBALL BATTING RULES

➡ Batters stand inside the batter's box and attempt to hit the ball and/or get on base.

➡ The *strike zone* is above home plate between the batter's armpits and knee tops when in a natural batting stance.

➡ Strikes are called when a batter:

- Swings at a pitch and misses.
- Does not swing at a ball pitched in the strike zone.
- Hits a foul ball on the first or second strike and the ball is not caught in the air by the fielders.
- Is hit by a pitch thrown into the strike zone.
- Is hit by a batted ball while standing in the batter's box with less than two strikes.

➡ The batter is out after three strikes.

➡ A *ball* is a pitch that does not pass through the strike zone and is not swung at by the batter.

➡ A batter is awarded first base (*walk* or *base on balls*) after four balls.

➡ If a batter does not swing at and is hit by a ball pitched outside of the strike zone, the batter is awarded first base.

➡ A *fair ball* is a batted ball that lands in or is touched by a player in fair territory, or lands in foul territory, then rolls fair into the infield.

➡ A *foul ball* is a batted ball that lands in or is touched by a player in foul territory, hits the bat or batter while in the batter's box, or rolls into and comes to rest in foul territory before reaching first or third base without being touched.

➡ The batter is out and any runners may try to advance to the next base if:

- The catcher catches a third strike.
- A fielder catches a third-strike foul ball.
- The batter swings and misses a third strike and is touched by the ball.
- There is a third strike with one out.
- A fly ball is caught.
- A fly ball is hit into the infield with runners on first and second base, or on first, second, and third with one out (*infield fly rule*).
- The batter does not reach first before the fielder touches base (*grounds out*) or is tagged out.

➡ The batter is out and the ball is not in play if:

- A fielder intentionally drops a fly ball with one out and a runner on base.
- A *bunt* (a ball lightly hit into the infield) goes foul after the second strike.
- The ball is hit twice.
- The batted ball hits the batter outside of the batter's box.
- The catcher drops a third strike but tags the batter with the ball or throws it to first before the batter reaches the base.
- The batter interferes with the catcher.
- While running to first base, the base runner interferes with a fielder's play.

➡ A *single* is a hit that allows the batter to safely reach first base.

➡ A *double* is a hit that allows the batter to safely reach second base.

➡ A *triple* is a hit that allows the batter to safely reach third base.

➡ A *homerun* is a hit that allows the batter to run safely around all the bases, cross home plate, and score a run.

➡ A *grand slam* is when there are runners on all three bases when a batter hits a homerun.

➡ The first batter in each inning is the next batter in the order after the last batter from the previous inning.

36. BASIC BASEBALL BASERUNNING RULES

➡ A runner may stay at a base until legally advancing to the next base or being forced to leave by the next baserunner.

➡ The runner must touch all bases in the correct order in order to score.

➡ Only one runner may be on a base at any one time.

➡ A baserunner may attempt to move to the next base if:

- A ball is hit into fair territory.
- After a fly ball is caught he or she *tags up* (touches the current base).
- He or she *steals* or runs to the next base as soon as the ball is pitched.

➡ A baserunner advances to the next base(s) with no risk of being put out if:

- The batter *walks*.
- A *balk* (pitching violation) is called on the pitcher.
- A ball in play is blocked.
- A ball in play is overthrown into out-of-play territory.
- A fielder obstructs a runner.
- A homerun is hit.
- A batter is awarded a *ground rule double* (the ball bounces over a fair boundary obstruction or goes into a playable area).

➡ A run does not score if the third out is from a force out or when the batter is out before reaching first.

➡ A baserunner is called out if:

- The runner is forced to advance to the next base and a fielder tags the runner or touches the base before he or she arrives.
- The runner is not on base and is tagged by a fielder when the ball is in play.
- A runner runs past first base but turns towards second and is tagged.
- A runner runs more than three feet outside a baseline.
- A runner interferes with a fielder making a play.
- A runner is hit by a fair ball while not on base before it passes any infielder except the pitcher.
- A runner passes another runner.
- A runner leaves a base before a fly ball is caught and is tagged out before returning.
- A runner misses a base and the fielder tags the base or runner.
- A runner intentionally kicks the ball.

➡ A baserunner is not out if:

- The runner goes outside of the base path to avoid a fielding attempt.
- The fielder is not in total control of the ball when tagging the runner.
- The runner overruns first base without making a turn towards second.
- The runner is hit by a batted ball while standing on base.

37. BASIC BASEBALL PITCHING RULES

➡ Eight warm-up pitches are allowed before each inning or for a *relief pitcher* (replacement pitcher) during an inning.

➡ Pitchers must throw the ball to the catcher within 20 seconds after receiving it.

➡ A *windup* is a legal starting position that consists of the following:

- The pitcher faces the batter.
- The pitcher's pivot foot touches the pitching plate and the other foot may be placed anywhere.
- The pivot foot may come off the rubber and the pitcher may throw to any base before the pitch.
- Once begun, the pitching motion must be continuous.
- The pivot foot may not leave the ground during the pitch.
- The free foot may take one step forward and backward during the pitch.

➡ A *set* is a legal starting position, which consists of the following:

- The pitcher faces the batter from a sidewards stance.
- The pitcher's pivot foot is on the rubber.
- The pitcher's free foot is in front of the rubber.
- The pitcher holds the ball in both hands in front of the body.
- The pitcher may bring the arms over the head but must come to a complete stop before pitching the ball.
- The motion to the plate may not be broken.

➡ *Pitching violations* include:

- Intentionally throwing a ball at a batter.
- Putting a foreign substance on the ball.
- Purposely damaging a ball.
- Throwing the ball to a base while the foot is still on the pitcher's plate.

➡ A *balk* is a pitching violation with runners on base that includes:

- Pitching when the foot is not in contact with the rubber.
- Pitching from the set position without coming to a full stop.
- Throwing to a base from the set position without first taking a step towards the base.
- Faking the throw to the batter or first base.
- Dropping the ball during the pitching motion.
- Not completing a pitch.
- Making a quick pitch.
- Delaying the game.

38. HISTORICAL FACTS ABOUT BASKETBALL

➡ Invented in 1891 by Dr. James Naismith, an instructor at the YMCA Training School in Springfield, Massachusetts.

➡ Specifically created to stimulate winter attendance at the YMCA.

➡ The game got its name from the two half-bushel peach baskets that were attached to the gymnasium balcony.

➡ The peach baskets were attached 10 feet above the floor and established a measurement that remains in use today.

➡ The original game began with 13 basic rules that are the foundation of the modern game.

➡ Women's basketball competition began in 1892.

➡ A player from the first women's team later married Dr. Naismith.

➡ A metal ring with a netted bag was used in place of the basket in 1893.

➡ The ball had to be released by pulling on a metal chain after each goal.

➡ Nets without bottoms were not introduced until 1913.

➡ Backboards were first used in 1894 to keep spectators from reaching out to deflect the ball.

➡ The game was originally played with 9 players on a team (Dr. Naismith had 18 students in his class).

➡ Five players on a team has been the standard since 1895.

➡ The first college game was in 1896 between Chicago and Iowa.

➡ The first professional game was in 1898.

➡ The National Basketball Association (NBA) was formed in June of 1946.

➡ In November of 1946, the NBA's first game was played at Maple Leaf Gardens with the New York Knickerbockers beating the Toronto Huskies, 68–66.

➡ The Women's National Basketball Association (WNBA) was formed in 1997.

39. ORIGINAL 13 BASKETBALL RULES FROM 1891

Here are the original 13 rules from 1891, written by Dr. James Naismith, the man who invented basketball.

1. The ball may be thrown in any direction with one or both hands.

2. The ball may be batted in any direction with one or both hands (never with the fist).

3. A player cannot run with the ball. The player must throw it from the spot on which he catches it, allowance to be made for a man who catches the ball at a good speed if he tries to stop.

4. The ball must be held in or between the hands. The arms or body must not be used for holding it.

5. No shouldering, holding, pushing, tripping, or striking of an opponent shall be allowed in any way. The first infringement of this by any player shall count as a foul; the second shall disqualify him until the next goal is made; or, if there was evidence of intent to injure the player, for the whole of the game. No substitutes allowed.

6. A foul is striking at the ball with the fist, violation of rules 3, 4, and such as described in rule 5.

7. If either side makes three consecutive fouls, it shall count as a goal for the opponents (consecutive means without the opponents in the meantime making a foul).

8. A goal shall be made when the ball is thrown or batted from the ground into the basket and stays there, providing those defending the goal do not touch or disturb the goal. If the ball rests on the edges and the opponents move the basket, it shall count as a goal.

9. When the ball goes out of bounds, it shall be thrown into the field of play by the person first touching it. In case of a dispute, the umpire shall throw it straight into the field. The thrower-in is allowed five seconds; if he holds it longer, it shall go to the opponent. If any side persists in delaying the game, the umpire shall call a foul on that side.

10. The umpire shall be the judge of men and shall note the fouls and notify the referee when three consecutive fouls have been made. He shall have the power to disqualify men according to rule 5.

11. The referee shall be the judge of the ball and shall decide when the ball is in play, inbounds, to which side it belongs, and shall keep time. He shall decide when a goal has been made, and keep account of the goals with any other duties that are usually performed by a referee.

12. The time shall be 15-minute halves, with five minutes rest between.

13. The side making the most goals in that time shall be declared the winner. In case of a draw, the game may, by agreement of the captains, be continued until another goal is made.

40. BASKETBALL EQUIPMENT

Ball

The official ball is spherical (round) with a circumference of 29 1/2 to 30 inches for men and 25 1/2 to 29 inches for women. The men's ball weighs 20 to 22 ounces and the women's ball weighs 18 to 20 ounces. Leather balls are used in competition, but balls are also made of rubber or synthetic materials.

Basket

The basket consists of a simple metal ring that is 18 inches in inside diameter and is secured to a backboard made of rectangular or fan-shaped glass, wood, or fiberglass. A white cord net is suspended beneath the ring from 12 hooks.

41. BASKETBALL BACKBOARD

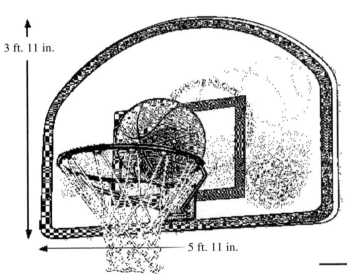

3 ft. 11 in.

5 ft. 11 in.

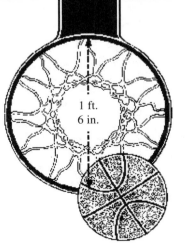

1 ft. 6 in.

42. BASKETBALL COURT

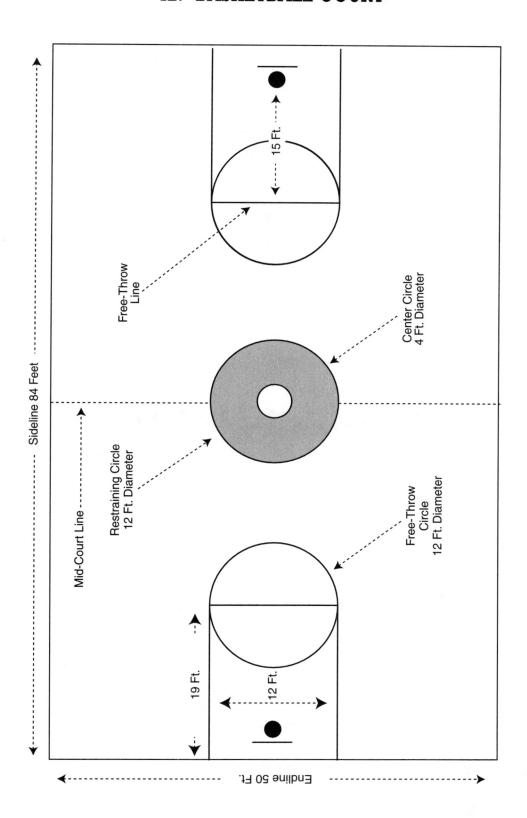

Sideline 84 Feet

Mid-Court Line

Free-Throw Line

15 Ft.

Center Circle 4 Ft. Diameter

Restraining Circle 12 Ft. Diameter

Free-Throw Circle 12 Ft. Diameter

19 Ft.

12 Ft.

Endline 50 Ft.

43. BASKETBALL POSITIONS

➡ Five team players usually include a *center,* two *guards,* and two *forwards.*

➡ The *center* (post, pivot) is usually the tallest player. He or she often takes the jump balls and is responsible for rebounding and close-range shooting.

➡ *Guards* are usually the best ball handlers. They advance up the court by dribbling and passing. The *point guard* sets up a team's offensive pattern like a quarterback.

➡ *Forwards* are responsible for shooting and rebounding missed shots.

➡ Extra players on the bench can substitute for the players on the court.

44. BASIC RULES OF BASKETBALL

Although there are rule variations between men and women's basketball and between the various levels of play, there are basic rules that govern play at any level.

➡ Only five players play on each team at one time.

➡ Any number of substitutions may be made during any dead ball.

➡ Substitutions must wait by the scorer's table until called into the game by an official.

➡ Any player may request a timeout.

➡ A goal is scored when the ball passes through the basket from above.

➡ Two points are scored for a goal from the court other than from the three-point area.

➡ Each successful free throw awarded for fouls scores one point.

➡ If a player puts the ball into the basket of the opponent, a goal is scored for the opponent.

➡ A total of five 1-minute timeouts may be taken and may be requested any time by the team in possession of the ball or by either team during a dead ball.

➡ If the score is tied at the end of regulation, play continues for as many extra periods are needed to break the tie.

→ The clock is stopped when an official indicates a dead ball.

→ The clock continues to run after successful field goals.

→ The ball is put into play at the beginning of the game by a jump ball in the center circle by two opposing players.

→ After each goal, the ball is put into play by the team that did not score the goal from behind the endline at the end of the court where the basket was scored.

→ Quarters and the half start with the team entitled to possession given the ball at the center division line.

→ A player is out-of-bounds when touching the floor on or outside of the boundary lines.

→ The ball is out-of-bounds when it touches a person or thing that is on or outside the boundary or the supports or back of the backboard.

→ A team is awarded a throw-in at the place where the opposing team caused the ball to go out-of-bounds.

→ An offensive player may not remain in the free-throw lane (the area between the endline, free-throw line, and free-throw lane lines) for more than 3 seconds during play.

→ If two opponents are both holding the ball, or if an offensive ball handler traps a defensive player for more than 5 seconds, the ball is awarded out-of-bounds to the team who did not last have the ball out-of-bounds.

→ Violations include:

- Sending the ball out-of-bounds
- Double dribbling
- Running with the ball
- Kicking the ball
- Striking the ball with the fist
- Interfering with the basket (goaltending)
- Stepping on the line during the throw-in
- Taking more than 5 seconds for a throw-in
- Staying in the free-throw lane for more than 3 seconds
- Keeping the ball in backcourt for more than 10 seconds

45. BASKETBALL FOULS

Personal fouls are violations involving contact with an opponent.

➡ A player is disqualified and removed from play after 5 personal fouls (6 in the NBA).

➡ Some personal fouls include:

- Holding, pushing, tripping, or charging
- Contact with a shooting player
- Rough play

➡ A player fouled while shooting is awarded 2 free throws if the shot misses.

➡ If the fouled offensive player is not shooting, the team gets possession out-of-bounds nearest where the foul occurred.

➡ The defensive team gets possession of the ball when the offensive team commits the foul.

➡ An intentional foul results in 2 free throws.

➡ A flagrant foul (violent contact that may cause injury) is awarded 2 free throws and the offender is ejected from the game.

A technical foul is a noncontact foul by a player or a violation by a nonplayer or an intentional or flagrant foul during a dead ball.

➡ Technical fouls include:

- Delay of game
- Having too many players on the court
- Grabbing the basket
- Excessive timeouts
- Goaltending free-throws
- Disrespectful behavior to officials
- Using profanity or obscene gestures
- Leaving the bench
- Coach leaving the box to follow the play
- Coach entering the court without permission

➡ Technical fouls are awarded 2 free throws, plus possession of the ball at the division line.

46. LENGTH OF BASKETBALL GAMES

The length of basketball games varies according to the level of play.

➡ International Basketball Federation (FIBA, Federation Internationale De Basketball Amateurs): two 20-minute halves, 10 minutes between halves

➡ National Basketball Association (NBA): four 12-minute quarters, 15 minutes between halves, 130 seconds between quarters

➡ National Collegiate Athletic Association (NCAA): two 20-minute halves, 15 minutes between halves

➡ High School: four 8-minute quarters, 10 minutes between halves, 1 minute between quarters

➡ Youth Play: four 6-minute quarters, 10 minutes between halves, 1 minute between quarters

47. BASKETBALL TERMS

Baseline	The endline.
Blocking Out (Boxing Out)	When a player positions him- or herself under the backboard in such a way that it prevents the opposition from achieving good rebounding position.
Charging	Personal contact against a defensive player by a player in possession of the ball.
Cut	Quick offensive maneuver by a player in order to get in position to receive a pass.
Double Foul	Two opposing players commit fouls against each other at the same time.
Dribble	Continuously bouncing the ball onto the floor without touching the ball with both hands at the same time, allowing the ball to stop its continuous movement, or losing control.
Drive	Aggressive move towards the basket by an offensive player in possession of the ball.
Fake (Feint)	Use of a deceptive move to pull the opposing player out of position.
Fastbreak	Moving quickly into offensive position before the defensive team has an opportunity to set up.

Free Throw	A penalty shot awarded to a player when the opposition has committed a foul. Shot is taken from within the free-throw circle and behind the free-throw line.
Jump Ball	Method of putting the ball into play that involves tossing the ball up into the air between two opposing players in the center circle.
Outlet Pass	Direct pass from a rebound that starts a fast break.
Pick	An offensive player gets in a position that causes a defensive player to be blocked from covering the offensive player's teammate.
Posting Up	Cutting to the 3-second lane and hesitating in anticipation of the pass.
Rebound	Term used for the action of the ball as it bounces off the backboard or rim.
Restraining Circles	Three 6-foot radius circles located in the center of the court and at both of the free-throw lines.
Screen	Offensive player gets in a position between a defender and a teammate in order to give the teammate an uncontested shot at the basket.
Throw In	Putting the ball into play from out-of-bounds.
Traveling	Player in possession of the ball moves illegally in any direction.

48. HISTORICAL FACTS ABOUT BOCCE

➡ A game resembling bocce is depicted in Egyptian artifacts from 4000 B.C.

➡ Graphic representations of figures tossing a ball or polished stone have been recorded as early as 5200 B.C.

➡ Armies under Alexander the Great introduced the game throughout Asia Minor, North Africa, and Italy.

➡ Early Romans were among the first to play the game, at times using coconuts brought back from Africa.

➡ The game continued to spread during the Roman Empire.

➡ Later on, hard olivewood was used to carve out bocce balls.

➡ There are indications that bocce was enjoyed by such luminaries as the emperor Augustus.

➡ Charles IV (Holy Roman Emperor) banned the game in the mid-fourteenth century so his subjects would concentrate on war.

➡ Throughout the centuries, the game enjoyed rapid growth as one of Europe's most popular pastimes.

➡ At one point in history several governments began to regulate its usage because it was found that the popularity of the game interfered with the security of the state.

➡ Kings Carlos IV and Carlos V prohibited the playing of bocce (citing national security).

➡ James I noted that bocce (*bowls*) was one of the few games permitted on the Sabbath.

➡ Medical docents from the University of Montpellier, France, claimed that playing bocce had great therapeutic effect in curing rheumatism.

➡ The Republic of Venice publicly condemned it on December 11, 1576, and thereafter those who disobeyed were punished with fines and imprisonment.

➡ The Catholic Church officially prohibited any clergyman from playing the game by declaring bocce a gambling device.

➡ Sir Francis Drake refused to interrupt his game to address a threatening military advance. "First we finish the game, then we'll deal with the Armada," it is believed he shouted to those who tried to hurry him on.

➡ The sport of bocce was excluded from the first modern Olympic Games held in Athens in April, 1896.

➡ Fifteen Piedmont Region teams formed the first organized Italian League on November 15, 1947 in the town of Rivoli.

➡ Since 1947, the Bocce World Championships have been held every year with France and Italy as the most prominent competitors.

➡ The game of bocce was organized competitively in the United States at the turn of the twentieth century.

➡ A strong influencing factor was the European immigration to the American continent.

➡ Early immigrants, trying to retain their original lifestyle, played the game as a way of duplicating the social environment they left behind.

➡ The oldest women's bocce league in this country (the Chisholm Women's Bocce League) started in 1944 with 25 women from Chisholm, Minnesota.

➡ Today the top three most-participated sports in the world are soccer, bocce, and golf.

49. BOCCE EQUIPMENT

➡ *Bocce balls* are made of wood or synthetic material and are identified by color or other markings. The official size bocce ball:

- Diameter—4 $\frac{1}{5}$ inches
- Circumference—13 $\frac{1}{2}$ inches
- Weight—2 lb. 2 oz.

➡ The *target ball* (*pallino* or *jack*) is made of wood or synthetic material and is 1 $\frac{3}{8}$ to 2 $\frac{1}{4}$ inches in diameter.

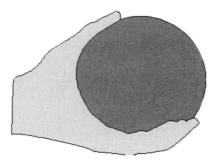

50. BOCCE COURT

The game of bocce is usually played on a hard, level surface of packed dirt or, ideally, a clay/sand and brick dust mixture. While a recreational game can be enjoyed on any available level surface, the ideal playing area should be a specially constructed court. Recommended court dimensions: a rectangular space measuring 80 ft. by 12 ft., skirted by a continuous railing of 4.5 to 12-inch high wood planking. Both ends of the playing area should be contained by higher walls to protect spectators from tossed balls.

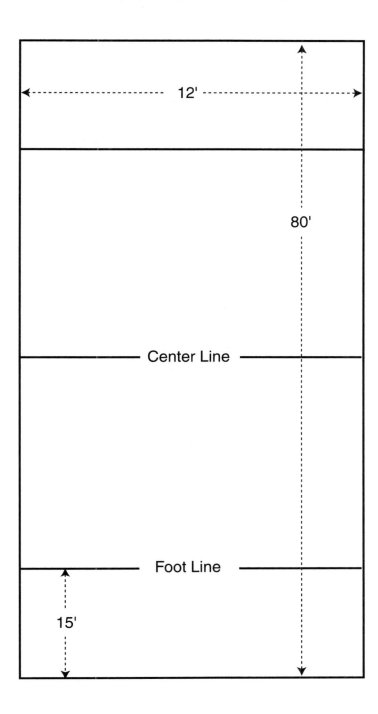

51. BASIC RULES OF BOCCE

➡ You need two equal teams to play bocce, with either one, two, or four persons per team. On a four-member team, two players from each side are stationed at opposite ends of the court and play alternate frames or innings.

➡ Once a team has been selected to go first, a player from that team begins by tossing the pallino anywhere towards the end of the court over the center line, then rolling or tossing one of the larger balls as close to the pallino as possible.

➡ The starting team does not bowl again until the opposing team has succeeded in getting one of its large balls closer to the pallino. The teams continue this way, with individual players alternating, until one side has used up all its balls, whereupon the other side is entitled to bowl its remaining balls. This ends a frame. Play switches to the opposite side of the court with each frame.

➡ One point is awarded to a given team for every ball that is closer to the pallino than the closest ball of the opposing team. The team that wins a frame on points starts play in the next frame. A game is 12 points.

➡ Balls are delivered underhand or overhand, in one of two motions: They can be tossed through the air or bowled. The ball must leave the hand before the player oversteps the foot line.

➡ Strategies can include knocking away an opponent's ball, knocking the pallino to change its position, and bank shots off the wooden court walls.

52. THREE BASIC BOCCE PLAYING METHODS

The traditional game of bocce calls for three basic styles or methods of play: the puntata (or "gentle" method), the volo (or "strong flying" method), and the raffa ("strong smash" method). Experience, ability, strategy, and personal preference are the factors that will determine your method of choice.

The Puntata Method

➡ This method is the most widely used.

➡ It is of particular advantage where the court surface is smooth, level, and generally free of debris.

➡ The player delivers the ball in a crouched position so that the ball is released in a slow rolling motion.

➡ This method requires a gentle touch.

➡ The bocce ball is rolled as close to the target ball as possible with a minimum of force.

➡ Best used early in play when there are no other balls to block the path to the target.

The Volo (Air Shot) Method

➡ Requires that the bocce ball be tossed high in the air with a reverse spin at the moment of release.

➡ This spin will cause the ball to stop at the point of impact.

➡ The volo player must not only gauge the proper distance but also the degree of spin that will produce the most effective shot.

➡ The volo is referred to as the strong or "smash" method because it is not delivered with the gentle motion of the puntata.

The Raffa (Strong) Shot Method

➡ One popular type of a "smash" shot is referred to in Italian as the raffa.

➡ The raffa is a strong shot like the volo shot, except that it is executed close to the ground.

➡ Its purpose is to dislodge an opponent's ball or to disrupt a well-placed formation.

53. HISTORICAL FACTS ABOUT BOWLING

→ Bowling is one of the oldest and most widely played of the world's games.

→ Its history has been traced back to the Stone Age, and to the Egyptians and Romans.

→ The earliest record of bowling goes back 7,000 years to ancient Egypt where a round object resembling a bowling ball, and marble bars, resembling bowling pins, were found in the ruins of a pyramid.

→ From Egypt, bowling moved to ancient Babylonia and then to Northern Italy around Julius Caesar's time.

→ The Italian version of bowling, *bocce,* which is still played today, is somewhat similar to lawn bowling—an English game originating over 800 years ago.

→ The English also played other games, such as half-bowls, skittles, and nine pins, which can be considered variations of bowling.

→ Bowling at pins was first mentioned in a book about the city of London, England, written over 800 years ago.

→ The first indoor bowling took place in London in 1455.

→ In Germany, the name of the game was *kegling* and the participants were known as "keglers."

→ Bowling came to America with the first Dutch settlers.

→ Washington Irving wrote about bowling in his famous story about Rip Van Winkle.

→ It was originally played with 9 pins in Europe.

→ According to popular legend, the tenth pin was added to circumvent a ruling in the 1840s by the Connecticut Legislature, which outlawed nine pins because of widespread gambling in the game.

→ The automatic pinspotter was introduced in the 1940s.

→ One out of every three Americans bowls.

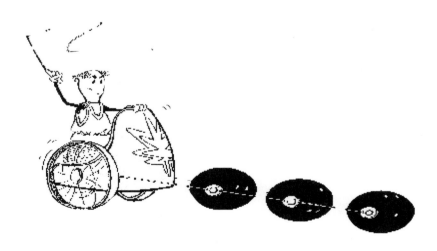

54. BOWLING EQUIPMENT

➡ *Bowling ball:* Made of rubber composition or plastic, it measures $8\frac{1}{2}$ inches in diameter and weighs 6 to 16 pounds. Although most balls have three finger holes, a maximum of five holes is permitted for the finger grip.

➡ *Bowling shoes:* Special shoes for bowlers have a sticky, rubbery sole on the nonsliding foot to act as a brake and a slicker, harder sole on the other foot to allow sliding on the last step.

55. POSITION AND NUMBERS OF BOWLING PINS

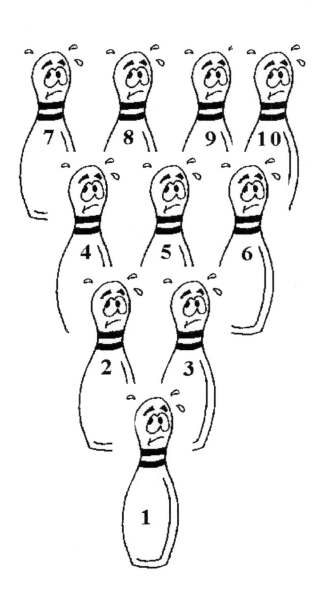

56. BOWLING LANE

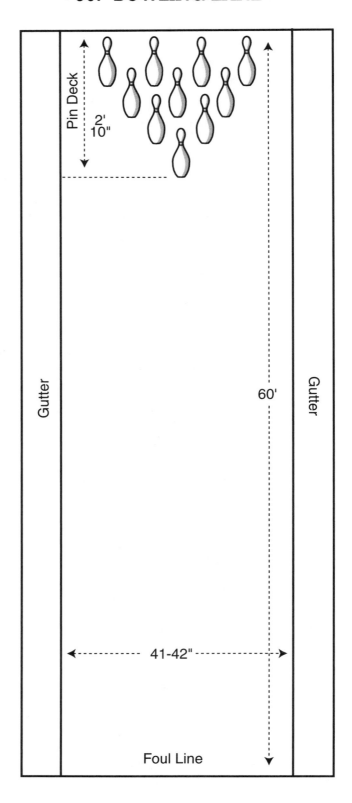

57. BASIC RULES OF BOWLING

→ Games may be played between individuals or teams.

→ Teams may have up to five players on a side.

→ A game consists of ten frames.

→ A bowler bowls a maximum of two balls each frame, with a possible exception of the tenth frame.

→ The ball must be rolled in an underhand motion.

→ The bowler cannot touch or cross the foul line.

→ Any pins knocked down by an illegally thrown ball do not count.

58. HOW TO SCORE BOWLING

→ There are ten numbered boxes on a score sheet that correspond to the ten frames in the game.

→ At the top of each frame box are one or two small squares in which to write the number of pins knocked over in that frame.

→ The score that is entered from frame box to frame box is cumulative (total number of pins knocked over up to that point).

→ With no spares or strikes, the score is simply a matter of adding up the number of pins knocked over each frame.

→ If all pins are knocked over with the first ball in the frame, it is a strike and an X is marked in the small square in the corner of the frame box.

→ The strike counts 10 points plus the number of pins knocked down on the next two consecutive balls thrown. The score is not entered until those two balls have been thrown.

→ If all the pins are knocked down with the next two balls, it is a spare and a diagonal line (/) is marked in the small square in the corner of the frame box.

→ The spare counts 10 points plus the number of pins knocked down on the next ball rolled. The score is not entered until the next ball has been rolled.

→ If a spare or strike is rolled in the tenth frame, one bonus ball is rolled for the spare and two bonus balls are rolled for a strike. The number of pins knocked down by the bonus balls is added to the score.

59. SYMBOLS USED TO SCORE BOWLING

X   Indicates a strike—10 plus the score of the next two balls.

/   Indicates a spare—10 plus the score of the next ball rolled.

O   Indicates a split—Score will depend on the number of pins knocked down by the next ball rolled.

Ø   Indicates a converted split—10 plus the score of the next ball rolled.

—   Indicates a miss or error; no score.

F   Indicates a foul; no score.

G   Indicates a gutter ball.

60. BOWLING TERMS

Alley	(1) A group of lanes; (2) bowling establishment; (3) playing surface, usually made of maple and pine boards.
Ball rack	(1) Where the ball rests before it is rolled and after it returns from the pit; (2) the structure used to store house balls.
Ball return	Track between the lanes the ball travels on when being returned to the bowler.
Bridge	Distance separating finger holes (as opposed to span, the distance between the thumb hole and middle finger hole).
Cushion	Padding at rear of pit to absorb shock of ball and pins.
Darts	The "arrows" located between 12 and 16 feet beyond the foul line; used for targeting.
Dots	Dots on the approach are used to set the bowler's feet at the start of the approach. Dots on the lane can be used to put the ball down on/toward or to swing through a visualized line between the dots and the arrows.
Foul line	The mark that determines the beginning of the lane, 60 feet this side of the head pin, where the gutters start. Crossing it gets a count of zero for that ball and, if on the first ball, a shot at a new rack of pins.
Four-step line	Usually a row of dots closest to the foul line; the dots farther back are for five-step deliveries.
Frame	Box in which the scores are entered (ten per game).
Gutter (or Channel)	Depression approximately $9\frac{1}{2}$ inches wide to the right and the left of the lane to guide the ball to the pit should it leave the playing surface.
Gutter ball	A ball that goes into the gutter.
Handicap	Pins awarded to individuals or teams in an attempt to equalize competition.

Headpin	The front or number 1 pin of a rack.
Kingpin	The headpin or the number 5 pin.
Lane	Playing surface. Wooden or urethane deck 62 feet $10^3/4$ inches long and 42 inches wide with ten pins spaced one-foot apart 60 feet from the foul line. Pins are on and gutters are at the side, not part of, the lane. Does not include the "approach."
Open	A frame that doesn't have a strike or spare. (Error, miss)
Perfect game	Twelve strikes in a row with a count of 30 pins per frame resulting in a score of 300.
Pin deck	Area 60 feet from the foul line where pins stand; usually has dark-colored spots where the pins are aligned.
Pit	Space at end of the lane where ball and pins wind up.
Return	The track on which balls roll from pit to ball rack.
Snake eyes	The 7–10 split. (Also called fence posts, goal posts, mule ears.)
Span	Distance between thumb and finger holes.
Spare	All pins down with two balls.
Split	A spare in which the headpin is down and the remaining combination of pins have an intermediate pin down immediately ahead of or between them. (Also called railroad.)
Strike	All ten pins down on the first ball.
300 game	A perfect game consisting of 12 strikes in a row.
Web	Distance between the finger holes, usually $1/4$ to $3/8$ of an inch. (Bridge)

61. HISTORICAL FACTS ABOUT DANCE

The origins of many dances are unclear, and often there aren't really any origins: Dances often grow out of each other. Dancing probably began as an imitative act, i.e., early people imitating some of the ritualistic dances of the animals. Historically, dance seems to have reached its low point during the days of classical Greece. Then it was looked upon as an ignoble activity. Aristotle was supposed to have said, "No citizen should pursue these arts (music and dance) so far that he approaches professional status," and relegated such activities to slaves, freedmen, and foreigners. The great Roman, Cicero, said, "Nobody dances unless he is drunk or unbalanced mentally." Italy saw the return of dancing during the fifteenth century, but France may be said to be the Mother of the modern art.

THE FOX TROT

Invented for a stage routine in 1914 by Harry Fox, it became so popular that he started teaching it as a social dance. The main difference with respect to earlier dances was its alternation of quick and slow steps.

POLKA

Originally a Czech peasant dance, it is believed that it was invented by a peasant girl. By 1833 it had reached Prague, and from there it went on to Paris, the rest of the continent, and the U.S. It never became very popular in England. After the Second World War, Polish immigrants in the U.S. adopted the dance, although the name has nothing to do with Poland: Pulka is Czech for "half-step."

THE SQUARE DANCE

Square dancing has been around for centuries. It began in England and France and came to America early in the history of the New World. As the population spread westward, so also did square dancing—taking different forms as it went. The uniquely American contribution to this development was the caller, sometimes called the prompter because he prompted the dancers' memory of patterns they had learned. Modern square dancing began with the advent of public address equipment to allow changing dance patterns and the use of recorded music. Hundreds of new calls were created during a 20-year period.

SWING

The precise origins of swing are not clear, although in the 1910s there was a similar dance called the Texas Tommy. Then there was the Lindy Hop that originated in the Savoy Ballroom in Harlem, New York. The name refers to Charles Lindbergh's "hop" across the ocean in 1927. From this evolved the Jitterbug. This name appears in a Cab Calloway song of the early 1930s. Lindy and Jitterbug evolved into East Coast Swing and Jive. West Coast Swing became a separate dance in the 1940s.

THE TANGO

The tango originated in Buenos Aires, Argentina, in the nineteenth century. A form of this tango was introduced in Spain and France at the end of the nineteenth century and in England at the start of the twentieth. Maurice Mouvet, a New Yorker of Belgian descent, learned this tango in Paris, and introduced it in New York in 1911, where it became an instant hit.

THE TWO-STEP

Dances carrying the name "Two Step" have existed since the nineteenth century, when it was done as a cowboy dance. There was a dance in the early 1800s called the "valse a deux temps" (two-beat waltz) which was rejected by many as appearing jerky in its movement. In 1847, in his book *La Danse des Salons*, Henri Cellarius expressed his regrets about the use of the term "deux temps," stating that the dance would be better accepted if it were called "deux pas" (two-step) as the term better described the step of the dance. Subsequent to his use of the term, many other authors used the term "two step."

THE WALTZ

The waltz was originally an Austrian peasant's dance, and was danced at the Hapsburg court in the seventeenth century. The current waltz grew out of a figure in the contredance. It was becoming accepted in high society by the start of the nineteenth century, though not without opposition from dance masters, clergy, and other guardians of public morals.

62. MOVEMENTS COMMON TO ALL DANCES

All forms of locomotion can be reduced to five fundamental steps  that include the walk, run, leap, jump, and hop. All other types of locomotion, including the skip, gallop, and slide, are a combination of these basic steps.

Walk   Weight is alternately transferred from one foot to the other with one foot always staying in contact with the ground.

Run   Speed of the walk is increased with a brief period when both feet are off the ground.

Leap   A spring into the air by means of a strong push off from one foot and returning to the ground on the other foot for the purpose of height or distance.

Jump   A spring into the air from both feet and landing on two feet. Other jumps may involve a single foot takeoff with a two-foot landing or a two-foot takeoff with a one-foot landing. A jump may be made for either height or distance.

Hop   A spring into the air by means of a strong push off from one foot and returning to the ground on the same foot.

Skip   A combination of a step and a hop. The free leg will swing forward and upward.

Slide   A sideward movement resulting from weight being transferred from one foot to the other with a step on one foot followed by a quick drawing up of the other foot with an immediate step and transfer of weight back to the first foot.

Gallop   Similar to a slide except with a forward movement of a step with one foot and then a leap with the other. The foot executing the leap is brought up to but not beyond the foot that has completed the step. The leap is completed with slight height; distance is not a factor.

63. DEFINITIONS OF DANCE, RHYTHM, AND METER

Meter Refers to time in music or grouping of beats to form the underlying rhythm within a measure.

Rhythmic Pattern The melody patterns or groupings of beats, as the melody of a song correspond to the underlying rhythm.

Even Rhythm Beats getting full note value, either long or short, causing a slow or fast rhythm.

Uneven Rhythm A combination of slow and quick beats.

Broken Rhythm A combination of slow and quick beats when the rhythm pattern takes more than one measure. A repetition will begin in the middle of a measure.

Tempo Rate of speed at which the music is played.

Measure One group of beats made by the regular occurrence of the heavy accent. It represents the underlying beat enclosed between two adjacent bars on the musical staff.

Phrase A musical sentence that can be felt by listening for the complete thought, similar to the way sentences may express a thought in a paragraph.

64. BASIC DANCE STEPS

Shuffle Moving forward with an easy one-step from one foot to the other. Different from a walk in that the weight is transferred from the ball of the foot to the heel or kept on the balls of the feet.

Two-Step Step forward on the left foot, close right to left, take weight on right, step left again. Repeat beginning with the right foot. The rhythm is uneven (quick, quick, slow) in 2/4 or 4/4 meter.

Polka A bright, lively dance in uneven rhythm (2/4 meter). Similar to a two-step with the addition of a hop so that it becomes hop-step-close-step with the hop coming on the up beat.

Schottische Three running steps and a hop or a step, close, step, hop done in a slow even rhythm (4/4 meter). Done in four measures (step step step hop, step step step hop, step hop, step hop, step hop, step hop). Common variations include holding, turning, or swinging the free leg on the fourth count instead of the hop.

Waltz A smooth, graceful dance step in an even three-beat rhythm consisting of three steps (step forward on the left, step to the side with the right, close left to right taking weight on left). Done in 3/4 meter with the accent on the first beat, the box waltz is the basic pattern for the box waltz turn (forward side close, backward side close).

Mazurka Step left, bring right up to left with a cut step displacing left, hop right while bending left knee so that left approaches the right ankle and repeat on the same side. Done in 3/4 meter using a strong, vigorous, even three-beat rhythm with the accent on the second beat.

65. SUGGESTIONS FOR TEACHING BASIC DANCE STEPS

Introduction of Basic Step Rhythm

➡ Explain and discuss accent, time signature, and rhythm and foot pattern in relation to rhythm.

➡ Have students listen to music.

➡ Clap rhythm with students.

➡ Write out rhythm and foot pattern in relation to rhythm on board.

Method of Presentation

➡ Walk through steps with analysis and demonstration.

➡ Have students practice steps.

➡ Apply the basic step in a simple sequence.

➡ Use the basic step in a simple dance.

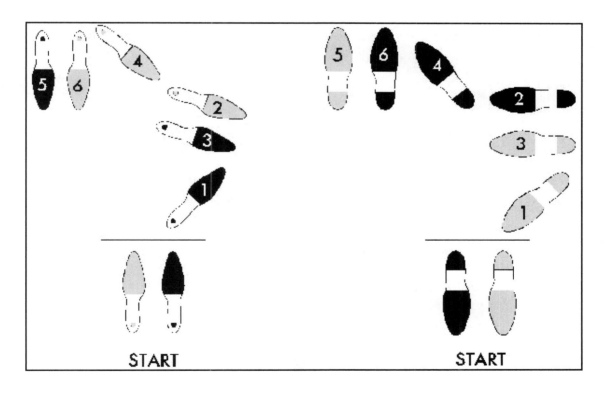

66. BASIC DANCE FORMATIONS

No Partner

- ➡ Single circle
- ➡ Broken circle
- ➡ Line, side by side
- ➡ File, one behind each other

Couples in a Circle

- ➡ Single circle, facing center
- ➡ Single circle, partners facing each other
- ➡ Double circle, couples facing each other
- ➡ Double circle, partners facing, one partner's back to center

Couples in a Line

- ➡ Side by side, facing forward
- ➡ Side by side, partners facing each other
- ➡ Side by side, alternate man and woman, facing forward
- ➡ Side by side, alternate man and woman, facing each other

Three People

- ➡ Three in a line, side by side
- ➡ Set of three, facing set of three
- ➡ Single circle, facing center

Two Couples

- ➡ Set of two couples, partners facing
- ➡ Set of two couples, couples facing

Four Couples

- ➡ Set of four couples, side by side, single circle, facing in

67. POSTURE IN RELATION TO DANCE

➡ Remain in an upright position, buttocks in, without leaning forward or backward.

➡ Avoid dragging your feet.

➡ Avoid planting your foot on each step.

➡ Transfer your weight smoothly and evenly from foot to foot.

➡ Avoid unnecessary side-to-side hip motion.

➡ Avoid unnecessary up-and-down body motion.

➡ Keep the feet and legs close together when possible.

➡ Practice walking backward while maintaining balance.

➡ Do not look at the floor or feet.

➡ Remain at ease but in complete control of the body.

➡ Relax, concentrate on the music, and enjoy the dance.

68. DANCE ETIQUETTE

→ Dress appropriately for the occasion to feel confident in your appearance.

→ Be attentive to partner.

→ Avoid looking around at others or acting bored.

→ Encourage your partner by covering up difficulties or ignoring weaknesses.

→ Work with your partner to generate a feeling of cooperation.

→ Ladies should always graciously accept a gentleman's request to dance.

→ A gentleman should not stand on the side or "cut in" if there is a lady waiting to dance.

→ A lady or gentleman should always graciously accept any partner with whom he or she is paired in a mixer.

→ Avoid singing, showing off, smoking, or gum chewing while dancing.

→ The gentleman should always take the lady's hand or arm to guide her to and from the dance floor.

→ Couples should move in a counterclockwise direction avoiding cutting across or moving in the opposite direction of traffic.

→ Avoid dances that require extra moving space while on a crowded dance floor.

→ Gentlemen should always thank a lady after the dance. Ladies should acknowledge the courtesy.

→ When couples are talking, it is courteous to introduce your partner.

→ Avoid teaching or asking to be taught new dance steps on the dance floor.

→ In square dancing, couples should introduce themselves.

→ Avoid leaving or changing a set after the sets have been formed.

→ A gentleman does not "cut in" on the gentleman who has taken his partner until another gentleman has cut in.

→ A lady should not refuse to change partners when a gentleman "cuts in."

→ A gentleman should touch the left shoulder of the lady's partner when "cutting in."

→ A gentleman should never leave a lady unaccompanied on the dance floor.

→ It is courteous to greet the hosts and guests at a dance.

→ It is courteous to thank the host and/or chaperones before leaving the dance.

69. HISTORICAL FACTS ABOUT FENCING

➡ The sport of sword fighting has existed since ancient Egypt.

➡ Jousting and tournament combat was a popular sport in the European Middle Ages.

➡ Unarmoured dueling forms evolved from sixteenth-century rapier combat.

➡ Rapiers evolved from cut-and-thrust military swords and spread from Spain and Italy to northwest Europe.

➡ By the eighteenth century, the rapier had evolved to a simpler, shorter, and lighter design that was popularized in France as the small sword.

➡ When buttoned with a leather safety tip that resembled a flower bud, the small sword was known as *le fleuret*, and was identical in use to the modern foil (still known as *le fleuret* in France).

➡ The French small-sword school forms the basis of most of modern fencing theory.

➡ By the mid-nineteenth century, dueling was in decline as a means of settling disputes, partially because victory could lead to a jail term for assault or manslaughter.

➡ Duels were fought over disputes that arose during Olympic games in the 1920s.

➡ In October 1997, the Mayor of Calabria, Italy, publicly challenged certain Mafiosos to a duel.

➡ The first modern Olympic games featured foil and saber fencing for men.

➡ Epee was introduced in 1900 and single stick was featured in the 1904 Olympic games.

➡ Epee was electrified in the 1936 games, foil in 1956, and saber in 1988.

➡ Until recently fencing was the only Olympic sport that included professionals.

➡ Women's foil was first contested in the 1924 Olympic games.

70. FENCING EQUIPMENT

Foil

➡ The foil, the modern version of the dueling rapier, has a flexible rectangular blade, approximately 35 inches in length, weighing less than one pound. Points are scored with the tip of the blade and must land within the torso of the body.

➡ The valid target area in foil is the torso, from the shoulder to the groin, front and back. It does not include the arms, neck, head, and legs. The foil fencer's uniform includes a metallic vest (called a lamé) which covers the valid target area, so that a valid touch will register on the scoring machine. A small, spring-loaded tip is attached to the point of the foil and is connected to a wire inside the blade. The fencer wears a body cord inside his uniform that connects the foil to a reel wire, connected to the scoring machine.

➡ There are two scoring lights on the machine. One shows a green light when a fencer is hit, and one shows a red light when the opponent is hit. A touch landing outside the valid target area (that which is not covered by the lamé) is indicated by a white light. These "off target" hits do not count in the scoring, but they do stop the fencing action temporarily.

Epee

➡ The epee (pronounced "EPP-pay"), the descendent of the dueling sword, is similar in length to the foil, but is heavier, weighing approximately 27 ounces, with a larger guard (to protect the hand from a valid hit) and a much stiffer blade. Touches are scored only with the point of the blade. The entire body is the valid target area.

➡ The epee is also an electrical weapon. The blade is wired with a spring-loaded tip at the end that completes an electrical circuit when it is depressed beyond a pressure of 750 rams. This causes the colored bulb on the scoring machine to light. Because the entire body is a valid target area, the epee fencer's uniform does not include a lamé. Off-target hits do not register on the machine.

Saber

➡ The saber is the modern version of the slashing cavalry sword, and is similar in length and weight to the foil. The major difference is that the saber is a point-thrusting weapon as well as a cutting weapon (use of the blade). The target area is from the bend of the hips (both front and back), to the top of the head, simulating the cavalry rider on a horse. The saber fencer's uniform includes a metallic jacket (lamé), which covers the target area to register a valid touch on the scoring machine. The mask is different from foil and epee, with a metallic covering since the head is a valid target area.

➡ Just as in foil, there are two scoring lights on the machine. One shows a green light when a fencer is hit, and one shows a red light when the opponent is hit. Off-target hits do not register on the machine.

Protective Wear

Mask Usually comes in small, medium, or large with a quilted, cotton canvas bib that attaches to the mask to protect the neck and throat.

Glove Usually made of leather with a padded gauntlet that is long enough to cover the end of the jacket sleeve for protection.

Jacket Sleeves of the jacket may not be too full but must provide underarm protection. A protective undergarment (plastron) must be worn and ladies must wear breast protectors.

71. FENCING PLAYING AREA

The playing area, called a piste, may be made of flat wood, linoleum, rubber, plastic, or metallic mesh and may be indoors or outdoors.

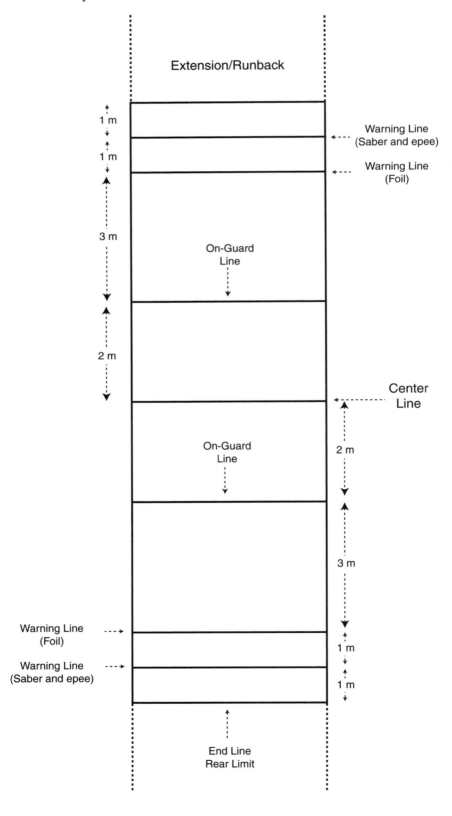

72. BASIC RULES OF FENCING

Object

→ The main object of a fencing bout (what an individual "game" is called) is to effectively score 15 points (in direct elimination play) or 5 points (in preliminary pool play) on your opponent before he or she scores that number. Each time a fencer scores a touch, he or she receives a point.

→ Direct elimination matches consist of three 3-minute periods.

Right-of-Way

→ This rule was established to eliminate simultaneous attacks by two fencers.

→ Right-of-way is the differentiation of offense and defense, made by the referee.

→ When both the red and green lights go on at the same time in foil and saber, the winner of the point is the one who the referee determined was on offense at the time the lights went on.

→ Epee does not use the right-of-way in keeping with its dueling origin. The fencer who first gains the touch earns the point.

→ If both fencers hit within $1/25$ of a second of each other, both earn a point.

73. FENCING SAFETY CONSIDERATIONS

→ Masks must be worn any time fencers face each other.

→ The tip of the foil must be covered with a rubber tip or protective tape.

→ Equipment must be checked often because blades are easily broken.

→ Discard masks that show rust or weak areas.

→ Fencing jackets should always be worn.

→ Discard jackets that are torn.

74. COMMON FENCING TERMS

Absence of blade   Blades are not touching; opposite of engagement.

Advance   Forward movement.

Assault   Friendly combat between two fencers.

Attack   Initial offensive action made by extending the sword arm and continuously threatening the valid target of the opponent.

Baudry point   Safety collar placed around a live epee point to prevent dangerous penetration.

Beat   Attempt to knock the opponent's blade aside or out of line by using one's foible or middle against the opponent's foible.

Bout   Assault at which the score is kept.

Button   Safety tip on the end of practice and sporting swords.

Cut   Attack made with a chopping motion of the blade.

Deception   Avoidance of an attempt to engage the blades.

Engagement   When the blades are in contact with each other.

En Garde (On Guard)   Fencing position; the stance that fencers assume when preparing to fence.

Epee   Fencing weapon with triangular cross-section blade and a large bell guard; also a light dueling sword of similar design, popular in the mid-nineteenth century.

Feint   Attack into one line with the intention of switching to another line before the attack is completed.

Foible   Upper, weak part of the blade.

Foil   Fencing weapon with rectangular cross-section blade and a small bell guard.

Forte   Lower, strong part of the blade.

Guard   Metal cup or bow that protects the hand from being hit; the defensive position assumed when not attacking.

Hilt   Handle of a sword, consisting of guard, grip, and pommel.

Invitation   Line intentionally left open to encourage the opponent to attack.

Lamé   Metallic vest/jacket used to detect valid touches in foil and saber.

Line   Main direction of an attack.

Lunge	Attack made by extending the rear leg and landing on the bent front leg.
Parry	Block of the attack, made with the forte of one's own blade.
Piste	Linear strip on which a fencing bout is fought; approx. 2 meters wide and 14 meters long.
Plastron	Partial jacket worn for extra protection.
Presentation	Offering one's blade for engagement by the opponent.
Rapier	Long, double-edged thrusting sword popular in the sixteenth and seventeenth centuries.
Right-of-way	Rules for awarding the point in the event of a double touch in foil or saber.
Saber	Fencing weapon with a flat blade and knuckle guard, used with cutting or thrusting actions; a military sword popular in the eighteenth through twentieth centuries.
Salute	Customary acknowledgment of one's opponent and referee at the start and end of the bout.
Thrust	Attack made by moving the sword parallel to its length and landing with the point.
Whites	Fencing clothing.

75. HISTORICAL FACTS ABOUT FIELD HOCKEY

➡ One of the oldest of competitive pastimes, the sport of field hockey dates back well before the Ancient Olympic Games.

➡ 4,000-year-old drawings found in the tomb at Beni-Hasen in the Nile Valley of Egypt depicted men playing the sport.

➡ Variations of the game were played by a spectrum of cultures ranging from Greeks and Romans to Ethiopians and Aztecs.

➡ The modern game of field hockey evolved in England in the mid-nineteenth century.

➡ The first men's hockey club, Blackheath, was formed in 1849, and led to the establishment of the Hockey Association in London in 1886.

➡ The British army introduced the game to India and throughout the British colonies, leading to the first international competition in 1895.

➡ Hockey first appeared on the Olympic program at the 1908 London Games and again in 1920 at Antwerp.

➡ By 1887, the first women's hockey club appeared in East Mosley, England, and was quickly followed by the creation of the All England Women's Hockey Association in 1889.

➡ The sport spread across the Atlantic in 1901 when English Physical Education instructor Constance Applebee introduced the sport to the U.S. while attending a seminar at Harvard.

➡ Appalled at the parlor games passing for exercise among young American women, Applebee borrowed some sticks and a ball and staged the first hockey exhibition in the United States behind the Harvard gymnasium.

➡ By the early 1920s, several colleges and clubs sponsored field hockey teams for women.

➡ In April of 1993, the FHAA and the USFHA, at the urging of the United States Olympic Committee, merged to form one national governing body for both women's and men's field hockey.

76. FIELD HOCKEY EQUIPMENT

Stick

➡ The stick consists of a straight handle with a curved head.

➡ The lower part of the stick's left-hand side (playing side) is smooth and flat.

➡ The back of the stick (right-hand side or nonplaying side) is smooth and rounded for the entire length of the stick.

➡ The stick is made of hardwood and is 36 to 38 inches long.

➡ Only the flat side of the stick may be used to strike the ball.

The Ball

➡ The ball is slightly larger than a baseball and weighs between $5\,1/2$ ounces and $5\,3/4$ ounces with a circumference of $8\,13/16$ inches to $9\,1/4$ inches.

➡ Usually white in color, other colors may also be used.

Goal Cages

➡ Goal cages are 7 feet (2.14 meters) high, 12 feet (3.66 meters) wide, and 4 feet (1.22 meters) deep.

➡ Boards on the back and side of the cages are 18 inches high.

Goalkeeper's Equipment

➡ Protective headgear includes a full helmet with full-face protection.

➡ Leg pads not to exceed 12 inches wide and hand protectors not to exceed 9 inches wide and 14 inches long.

77. FIELD HOCKEY FIELD

The playing field (pitch) is 100 yards by 60 yards (91.40 meters by 55.0 meters), divided by a center line and a 25-yard line on each half of the field. The striking circle is a semicircle measured out 16 yards from each goal post.

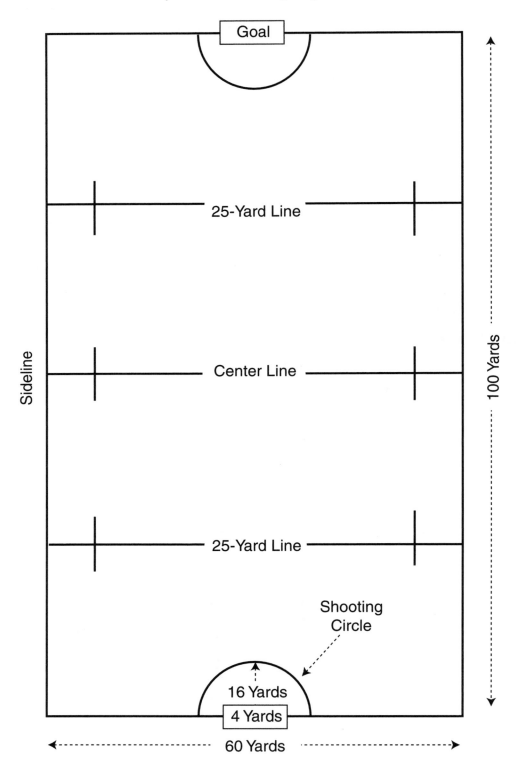

78. FIELD HOCKEY RULES

➡ The game consists of two halves, 35 minutes each in collegiate and international play, 30 minutes each in high school play.

➡ Eleven players per side, including the goalkeeper.

➡ Two umpires on the field officiate the match.

➡ A goal is scored when an attacker strikes the ball into the goal from within the striking circle.

➡ Players may not shield the ball using their body or stick.

➡ All players must have an equal chance to play the ball.

➡ Using sticks that are flat on one side and curved on the other, teams hit and dribble a solid ball down the field using the flat side of the stick and try to shoot it past a goalkeeper into a goal cage.

➡ Shots may only be taken from within the striking circle.

Extra Time/Overtime

➡ In *international* play for classification rounds or games that require a winner to advance to the next round, overtime of two $7\,1/2$-minute periods is played if the score is tied after regulation. The game is ended when one team scores a goal. If the score remains tied after overtime, penalty strokes may be used to determine the winner. In penalty-stroke competition, each team selects five players to take alternating penalty strokes against the opposing goalkeeper.

➡ In *high school federation* play, if the score is tied after regulation time has expired, an overtime period of two 10-minute halves is played with each team reducing the number of players to seven per side. If the score remains tied after overtime, penalty strokes may be used to determine the winner. In penalty-stroke competition, each team selects five players to take alternating penalty strokes against the opposing goalkeeper.

Fouls

A player may *not*:

➡ Shield or obstruct the ball from an opponent with the body or stick.

➡ Play the ball with the rounded side of the stick.

➡ Interfere in the game without a stick.

➡ Charge, hit, shove, or trip an opponent.

➡ Play the ball in a potentially dangerous way.

➡ Use the foot or leg to support the stick in order to resist an opponent.

➡ Raise the stick in a dangerous or intimidating manner while approaching or attempting to play or stop the ball.

➥ Advance the ball by any means other than with the stick.

➥ Stop or deflect the ball in the air or on the ground with any part of the body.

➥ Hit, hook, hold, or interfere with an opponent's stick.

Free Hit

➥ A free hit is awarded to the nonoffending side following an infraction and is usually taken at the spot the foul occurs.

➥ No player of the opposing team may be within five yards of the ball when hit.

➥ Ball must be stationary and the striker must push or hit it.

➥ Hitter may not replay the ball until another player has touched it.

➥ If the infraction is committed by a defender within the shooting circle, the attacking team is awarded a penalty corner.

Penalty Corner

➥ In a penalty corner, the ball is placed on the goal line at least 10 yards from the nearest goal post.

➥ One attacking player hits the ball to a teammate just outside the striking circle line.

➥ No shot on goal may be taken until the ball is stopped or comes to rest on the ground outside the circle.

➥ All attackers must be outside the circle before the hit is taken.

➥ On defense, a maximum of five defenders may be behind the goal line while the remaining defenders must be positioned beyond the center line.

➥ The attacking player taking the free hit passes the ball to her teammates positioned outside the striking circle.

➥ An offensive player will stop the ball with the stick while another player will strike the ball at the goal.

➥ A penalty corner is awarded for the following offenses:
  • Any breach of the rule by a defender within the circle that would have resulted in a free hit to the attacking team if the breach had occurred outside the circle.
  • Any intentional breach of the rule by the defenders outside the circle but within the 25-yard line.
  • An intentional hit over the goal line by a defender from any part of the field.

Penalty Stroke

➥ A penalty stroke is a one-on-one confrontation between an offensive player seven yards in front of the goal versus a goalkeeper on the goal line.

➥ All other players must stand behind the 25-yard line.

➡ The goalkeeper must stand with both feet on the goal line and may not move either foot until the ball has been played.

➡ The offensive player may push, flick, or scoop the ball from the penalty spot.

➡ A penalty stroke is awarded for any intentional breach by the defenders in the circle or for an unintentional breach by the defenders that prevents a sure goal.

16-Yard Hits

➡ When the attacking team plays the ball over the back line, the defense receives a 16-yard hit.

➡ The free hit is taken 16 yards from the spot where the ball crossed the back line.

The Push-In or Hit-In

➡ A push-in or hit-in is awarded to the opposition if a player hits the ball wholly over the sideline.

➡ All other players and their sticks must be at least five yards away from the spot where the ball is put into play.

Offenses and Misconduct

For rough or dangerous play, misconduct, or any intentional offense, the umpire may:

➡ Caution the offending player.

➡ Warn the offending player with a green card.

➡ Temporarily suspend the offending player for a minimum of 5 minutes with a yellow card.

➡ Permanently suspend the offending player with a red card.

79. SELECTING A FIELD HOCKEY STICK

Balance and Weight

➡ Field hockey sticks range in weight from light (18 oz. to 19 oz.), to medium (19–22 oz.), to heavy (22 oz. to FIH maximum 25.9 oz. [737 grams]). Most players will use a stick in the medium range. Generally, forwards prefer a lighter stick for quick maneuvering in the circle while defenders often choose a heavier stick for powerful clearing hits and to prevent attackers from casually "pushing" the stick aside. The weight in the toe should not be so much as to limit your stick speed when playing the ball.

Length of Stick

➡ Field hockey sticks range in length from 26- and 28-inch youth sticks to 38-inch sticks for taller and more experienced players. While the length of the stick is often determined by height, players often select the longest stick they can handle comfortably.

➡ The chart below shows the general guideline for choosing the appropriate length stick:

Height:	Up to 4'	4'–4'3	4'4–4'6	4'7–5'	5'1–5'3	5'4–5'6	5'7–5'8	5'9 +
Stick Length:	26"	28"	32"	34"	35"	36"	37"	38"

Toe Length

➡ The "shorti toe" features a one-piece head to allow quick maneuverability around the ball.

➡ The "midi toe" features an increased hook surface and slightly longer length to allow a larger hitting and stopping area to facilitate receiving, flicking, and reverse stick play.

➡ A "hook toe" hooks up to provide the maximum surface for receiving and a larger sweet spot for hitting.

Flexibility and Stiffness

➡ A flexible stick that absorbs shock is often the stick of choice for beginning or novice players. Flexible sticks tend to be more durable than their stiffer counterparts.

➡ Advanced players may opt for a stiffer stick for increased power.

80. FIELD HOCKEY TERMS

Bully   A neutral restart to play following a stop in the action. The ball is placed on the ground between two players, one from each team. The players tap the ground with their sticks, then tap their sticks together three times before going for the ball.

Center Pass   A pass back from the center of the field used to start the game or restart the action following a score.

Flick   A pushed ball that is raised off the ground.

Obstruction   An infraction for shielding the ball from an opponent with a player's body or stick. All players must have an equal chance to gain control of the ball as it is dribbled or passed down the field.

Penalty Corner A free hit awarded to an offensive player from a point on the goal line at least 10 yards from the nearest goal post. One attacking player hits the ball to a teammate just outside the striking circle line. No shot on goal may be taken until the ball is stopped or comes to rest on the ground outside the circle. All attackers must be outside the circle before the hit is taken. A maximum of five defenders may be behind the goal line while the remaining defenders must be positioned beyond the center line.

Pitch   The playing field. It is 100 yards by 60 yards, divided by a center line and a 25-yard line on each half of the field.

Push   Moving the ball along the ground by a pushing movement of the stick. Both the head of the stick and the ball are in contact with the ground.

Scoop   The lifting of the ball off the ground by placing the head of the stick under the ball and shoveling the ball forward.

Striking Circle or "Circle" A semicircle measured 16 yards from each goal line from which all goals must be struck.

81. TEN BENEFITS OF REGULAR EXERCISE (FITNESS)

1. Reduced risk of heart disease

2. Improved blood cholesterol levels

3. Prevention of high blood pressure

4. Boosted energy levels

5. Reduced stress and tension

6. Improved sleep patterns

7. Better self-image

8. Increased muscle strength, giving greater capacity for other physical activities

9. Provides a way to share an activity with family and friends

10. Establishes good, healthy habits in children and counters the conditions that lead to heart attack and stroke later in life (obesity, high blood pressure, poor cholesterol levels, poor lifestyle habits, etc.)

82. KEEPING CHILDREN PHYSICALLY FIT—TIPS FOR PARENTS

According to Don Tinder, *Golf Illustrated/Golf Digest* Contributing Fitness Writer, becoming active ourselves and paying attention to our children's habits is paramount to teaching our kids about the values and attributes behind becoming physically active. Here are some tips on how to keep children physically fit:

1. Try to limit your child's time spent watching television, movies, videos, and computer games to less than two hours a day. Substituting the rest of leisure time with physical activity will provide lasting benefits to a child.

2. Stay involved in your child's physical education classes at school. Ask about frequency of classes and activity, class size, curriculum (instruction in lifetime fitness activities as well as team sports should be emphasized), physical fitness assessments, and qualifications of the teacher (should hold appropriate certification in physical education and be an appropriate role model for students). Physical fitness should be measured at the beginning and end of each year, and goals should be established for each child.

3. Observe what sports and activities appeal to your child, then find out about lessons and clubs. Whatever you and your child take the time to participate in, try to gradually incorporate the benefits of physical fitness into his or her daily life.

4. Choose fitness-oriented gifts—a jump rope, mini trampoline, tennis racket, baseball bat, a youth membership at the local YMCA or YWCA. Select the gift with your child's skills and interests in mind.

5. If it is safe to walk or bike rather than drive, do so. Use stairs instead of elevators and escalators.

6. Spring your infant from mechanical restraints as much as possible. Strollers and playpens are high on convenience, but low on activity potential. Try to unleash your diapered dynamo whenever and wherever he or she can safely move around.

7. When your child is bored, suggest something that gets him or her moving—like playing catch or doing some work in the yard.

8. Allow your child to play immediately after school to allow him or her to find some diversion from the structure of the school day. Children should be active after school and before dinner. Don't forget, though, that homework must be done!

83. FACTS ABOUT WARMING UP AND COOLING DOWN

Warming Up

➡ The main purpose of warming up is to increase the heart rate slightly.

➡ Warming up raises the core body temperature. It increases the blood (oxygen) flow to the muscles to prepare the body for more vigorous physical activity.

➡ Muscles and tendons (which attach muscles to bones) will be more flexible for stretching after mild movement has raised the internal body temperature.

➡ Flexibility helps to increase the range of motion of the joints and may help to avoid injuries such as muscle tears and pulls.

➡ It takes the body approximately 3 minutes to realize it needs to pump more blood to the muscles.

➡ Warm-ups should last approximately 5 to 10 minutes and should incorporate stretching of large muscle groups (such as the quadriceps, calves, hamstrings, and shoulders).

Cooling Down

➡ After you've reached and maintained your training heart rate level, it is important to recover gently.

➡ The cool-down reduces the pulse. It returns the blood to the heart in sufficient quantities to rid the muscles of lactic acid (a chemical result of muscular fatigue).

➡ If the body stops suddenly, the blood will pool in the legs instead of returning to the heart.

➡ Dizziness, nausea, and a "worn out" feeling are common symptoms of an improper cool-down.

➡ It takes the body approximately 3 minutes to realize it does not need to pump all the additional blood to the muscles.

➡ A safe cool-down period is at least 3 minutes, preferably 4 to 5 minutes.

➡ All cool-downs should be followed by stretching of the muscles to avoid soreness and tightness.

84. BASIC STRETCHING EXERCISES (EXAMPLE 1)

STANDING CALF STRETCH

Lean against a wall, fence, etc., with the back leg straight, the front leg bent, and the feet pointing forwards. Ensure that the heel of the back leg remains on the ground. Leaning closer to the wall may increase the stretch. Additional stretch of the Achilles tendon may be achieved by bending the back leg. *Variation:* Have both legs together and straight, thus stretching both legs at the same time.

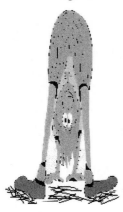

QUADRICEPS STRETCH

Stand on one leg, grasp the foot with the hand, and pull into the buttock. To increase the stretch, draw the knee back and extend the hip a little further. If balancing on one leg is difficult, it may be necessary to find a support such as a wall or partner.

STANDING GROIN STRETCH

Stand with the feet about a yard apart and pointing forward. Keeping one leg straight and the foot on the floor, bend the other knee and lean forwards.

STANDING SIDE STRETCH

Stand with feet a little more than shoulder-width apart and knees slightly bent. Reach one arm above the head and place the other hand on the thigh. If the right arm is raised, then bend slowly from the hips to the left side. Maintain body in the same plane. Repeat to the opposite side.

SHOULDER AND TRICEPS STRETCH

With the arms above the head, place one hand down the back and push on the elbow with the other hand.

UPPER BACK STRETCH

Take your right arm across your body at shoulder height and place your right hand around your back. With your left hand gently push your right arm further forward and around your body.

SHOULDER AND CHEST STRETCH

Extend both arms behind the back and interlock fingers. With the palms facing inwards, slowly raise the arms upward.

SIDE AND SHOULDER STRETCH

Interlace fingers and stretch arms above your head with the palms of the hands facing the top of the head. Slowly push hands slightly back and up.

85. BASIC STRETCHING EXERCISES (EXAMPLE 2)

It is important to stretch after doing a few minutes of aerobic activity, such as walking or marching in place. A warm muscle will stretch better, and is less likely to become injured. It is also just as important to stretch after you exercise.

ARM CIRCLES

Rotate both arms around slowly in an exaggerated manner, then try to round shoulders and then straighten them out.

CHEST STRETCH

After arm circles, try to bring hands towards each other behind the back, feeling a gentle stretch through the shoulder area.

HAMSTRING STRETCH

Stand with one leg extended in front of the other with the heel of that foot down and the toes up, and the other leg slightly bent, with arms on the hips. Gently lean forward, keeping torso and head up. Hold stretch 30 to 60 seconds. Alternate to other leg.

LUNGE STRETCH

Stand in lunge position with the front lead leg bent (keep toes in line with knee) and have back leg in a straighter position (still at a slight bend around knee). Keep hands on the hip and push down slightly with hips. A gentle stretch should be felt through the hip flexors. Hold for 30 to 60 seconds, then alternate to other side.

CALF STRETCH

Stand with back leg extended and heel flat on the floor. (Almost a lunge position.) Front leg is bent more. After holding this position 30 to 60 seconds, slightly bend the back leg while still keeping the heel flat on the floor. This will allow a stretch of the solius muscle, which is deep under the calf muscle. This stretch can also be done by standing on the edge of a step and letting the heel drop down lower than the toes.

HIP STRETCH

Stand up tall, then lean slightly to one side without bending forward at the waist. Hold, then alternate to the other side.

LOW BACK STRETCH

Lying on the ground, slowly bend one knee and pull it towards the chest while trying to keep the back flat against the floor. This stretches the outside part of hips as well as lower back. Alternate and stretch with other knee.

86. CALCULATING TARGET HEART RATE

The target heart rate is what your pulse rate should be to exercise safely and receive the maximum cardiovascular benefits. Heart rate is widely accepted as a good method for measuring intensity during running, swimming, cycling, and other aerobic activities. Exercise that doesn't raise your heart rate to a certain level and keep it there for 20 minutes won't contribute significantly to cardiovascular fitness.

The easiest way to check your heart rate is to place the tips of your middle and index fingers in the groove of your throat just to the side of the Adam's apple. Count the heartbeats for six seconds and multiply the number of beats by 10. If you are not within your range, you may need to adjust your workout. After cooling down, check your pulse rate again. It should be below 100 before you stop moving.

Target Heart Rate

➡ Lower Limit = (220 – age) ✕ 50% (lower limit)

➡ Upper Limit = (220 – age) ✕ 75% (upper limit)

The (220 – age) is actually an estimate of your maximum heart rate. In other words, your target heart rate during exercise should be about 50–75% of your maximum heart rate.

Calculate both the lower and upper limits to find your target heart rate zone. Your target heart rate falls within this zone. When your heart rate reaches a value within this zone during exercise, it means you have achieved a level of activity that contributes to your cardiovascular fitness. *Your heart rate during exercise should not exceed the upper limit of this zone!*

INDIVIDUALIZED TARGET HEART RATE

Some methods for figuring the target rate take individual differences into consideration. Here is one of them.

➡ Subtract your age from 220 to find maximum heart rate.

➡ Subtract resting heart rate (see below) from maximum heart rate to determine heart rate reserve.

➡ Take 70% of heart rate reserve to determine heart rate increase.

➡ Add heart rate increase to resting heart rate to find target heart rate.

RESTING HEART RATE

Find your resting heart rate by taking your pulse after sitting quietly for 5 minutes. Count your pulse for 10 seconds and multiply by 6 to get the per-minute rate.

87. PRESIDENTIAL FITNESS TEST STANDARDS

The President's Challenge is a physical fitness awards program of the President's Challenge on Physical Fitness and Sports (PCPFS). The program is for ages 6 through 17, including those students with special needs. The PCPFS recommends fitness testing at least twice a year, in the fall and the spring. Before performing the test, all students should be taught the correct techniques for all components. There is no limit to the number of attempts a student can have on each item. All five tests are required and must be performed in order for a student to qualify for an award. The Presidential Physical Fitness Award* participants must at least reach these levels in all five events in order to qualify for the Presidential Physical Fitness Award. These levels represent the 85th percentile based on the 1985 School Population Fitness Survey.

BOYS

AGE	CURL-UPS (# - 1 min.)	PARTIAL CURL (#)	SHUTTLE RUN (seconds)	V-SEAT REACH (inches)	SIT AND REACH (centimeters)	ONE MILE (min: sec)	DISTANCE OPT. 1/4 mile (min:sec)	DISTANCE OPT. 1/2 mile (min:sec)	PULL-UPS (#)	RT. ANGLE Pull-ups (#)
6	33	22	12.1	+3.5	31	10:15	1:55	N/A	2	9
7	36	24	11.5	+3.5	30	9:22	1:48	N/A	4	14
8	40	30	11.1	+3.0	31	8:48	N/A	3:30	5	17
9	41	37	10.9	+3.0	31	8:31	N/A	3:30	5	18
10	45	35	10.3	+4.0	30	7:57	N/A	N/A	6	22
11	47	43	10.0	+4.0	31	7:32	N/A	N/A	6	27
12	50	64	9.8	+4.0	31	7:11	N/A	N/A	7	31
13	53	59	9.5	+3.5	33	6:50	N/A	N/A	7	39
14	56	62	9.1	+4.5	36	6:26	N/A	N/A	10	40
15	57	75	9.0	+5.0	37	6:20	N/A	N/A	11	42
16	56	73	8.7	+6.0	38	6:08	N/A	N/A	11	44
17	55	66	8.7	+7.0	41	6:06	N/A	N/A	13	53

GIRLS

AGE	CURL-UPS (# - 1 min.)	PARTIAL CURL (#)	SHUTTLE RUN (seconds)	V-SEAT REACH (inches)	SIT AND REACH (centimeters)	ONE MILE (min: sec)	DISTANCE OPT. 1/4 mile (min:sec)	DISTANCE OPT. 1/2 mile (min:sec)	PULL-UPS (#)	RT. ANGLE Pull-ups (#)
6	32	22	12.4	+5.5	32	11:20	2:00	N/A	2	9
7	34	24	12.1	+5.0	32	10:36	1:55	N/A	2	14
8	38	30	11.8	+4.5	33	10:02	N/A	3:58	2	17
9	39	37	11.1	+5.5	33	9:30	N/A	3:53	2	18
10	40	33	10:8	+6.0	33	9:19	N/A	N/A	3	20
11	42	43	10.5	+6.5	34	9:02	N/A	N/A	3	19
12	45	50	10.4	+7.0	36	8:23	N/A	N/A	2	20
13	46	59	10.2	+7.0	38	8:13	N/A	N/A	2	21
14	47	48	10.1	+8.0	40	7:59	N/A	N/A	2	20
15	48	38	10.0	+8.0	43	8:08	N/A	N/A	2	20
16	45	49	10.1	+9.0	42	8:23	N/A	N/A	1	24
17	44	58	10.0	+8.0	42	8:15	N/A	N/A	1	25

*Award standards were most recently validated in 1998 by means of a comparison with a large nationwide sample collected in 1994.

88. NATIONAL PHYSICAL FITNESS AWARD STANDARDS*

BOYS

AGE	CURL-UPS (# - 1 min.)	PARTIAL CURL (#)	SHUTTLE RUN (seconds)	V-SEAT REACH (inches)	SIT AND REACH (centimeters)	ONE MILE (min: sec)	DISTANCE OPT. 1/4 mile (min:sec)	DISTANCE OPT. 1/2 mile (min:sec)	PULL-UPS (#)	RT. ANGLE Pull-ups (#)	FLEX ARM HANG (sec)
6	22	10	13.3	+1.0	26	12:36	2:21	N/A	1	7	6
7	28	13	12.8	+1.0	25	11.40	2:10	N/A	1	8	8
8	31	17	12.2	+0.5	25	11:05	N/A	4:22	1	9	10
9	32	20	11.9	+1.0	25	10:30	N/A	4:14	2	12	10
10	35	24	11.5	+1.0	25	9:48	N/A	N/A	2	14	12
11	37	26	11.1	+1.0	25	9:20	N/A	N/A	2	15	11
12	40	32	10.6	+1.0	26	8:40	N/A	N/A	2	18	12
13	42	39	10.2	+.0.5	26	8:06	N/A	N/A	3	24	14
14	45	40	9.9	+1.0	28	7:44	N/A	N/A	5	24	20
15	45	45	9.7	+2.0	30	7:30	N/A	N/A	6	30	30
16	45	37	9.4	+3.0	30	7:10	N/A	N/A	7	30	28
17	44	42	9.4	+3.0	34	7:04	N/A	N/A	8	37	30

GIRLS

AGE	CURL-UPS (# - 1 min.)	PARTIAL CURL (#)	SHUTTLE RUN (seconds)	V-SEAT REACH (inches)	SIT AND REACH (centimeters)	ONE MILE (min: sec)	DISTANCE OPT. 1/4 mile (min:sec)	DISTANCE OPT. 1/2 mile (min:sec)	PULL-UPS (#)	RT. ANGLE Pull-ups (#)	FLEX ARM HANG (sec)
6	23	10	13.8	+2.5	27	13:12	2:26	N/A	1	6	5
7	25	13	13.2	+2.0	27	12.56	2:21	N/A	1	8	6
8	29	17	12.9	+2.0	28	12.30	N/A	4:56	1	9	8
9	30	20	12.5	+2.0	28	11:52	N/A	4:50	1	12	8
10	30	24	12.1	+3.0	28	11:22	N/A	N/A	1	13	8
11	32	27	11.5	+3.0	29	11:17	N/A	N/A	1	11	7
12	35	30	11.3	+3.5	30	11:05	N/A	N/A	1	10	7
13	37	40	11.1	+3.5	31	10:23	N/A	N/A	1	11	8
14	37	30	11.2	+4.5	33	10:06	N/A	N/A	1	10	9
15	36	26	11.0	+5.0	36	9:58	N/A	N/A	1	15	7
16	35	26	10.9	+5.5	34	10:31	N/A	N/A	1	12	7
17	34	40	11.0	+4.5	35	10:22	N/A	N/A	1	16	7

*For students scoring at or above the 50th percentile on all five items of the President's Challenge.

89. PRESIDENTIAL PHYSICAL FITNESS TEST EVENTS

CURL-UPS

Objective: To measure abdominal strength/endurance by maximum number of curl-ups performed in one minute. *Testing:* Have student lie on cushioned, clean surface with knees flexed and feet about 12 inches from buttocks. Partner holds feet. Arms are crossed with hands placed on opposite shoulders and elbows held close to chest. Keeping this arm position, student raises the trunk, curling up to touch elbows to thighs, and then lowers the back to the floor so that the scapulas (shoulder blades) touch the floor, for one curl-up. To start, a timer calls out the signal "Ready? Go!" and begins timing student for one minute. The student stops on the word "stop." *Rules:* "Bouncing" off the floor is not permitted. The curl-up should be counted only if performed correctly.

PARTIAL CURL-UPS (OPTION TO CURL-UPS)

Objective: To measure abdominal strength/endurance by maximum number of curl-ups. *Testing:* Have student lie on cushioned, clean surface with knees flexed and feet about 12 inches from buttocks. The feet are *not* held or anchored. Arms are extended forward with fingers resting on the legs and pointing toward the knees. The student's partner is behind the head with hands cupped under the student's head. The student being tested curls up slowly, sliding the fingers up the legs until the fingertips touch the knees, then back down until the head touches the partner's hands. The curl-ups are done to a metronome (or audio tape, clapping, drums) with one complete curl-up every three seconds, and are continued until the student can do no more in rhythm (has not done the last three in rhythm) or has reached the target number for the PPFA. *Scoring:* Record only those curl-ups done with proper form and in rhythm. *Rationale:* The partial (abdominal) curl-ups, done slowly with knees bent and feet not held, replace the timed curl-ups because they are a better indicator of the strength and endurance of the abdominal muscles.

SHUTTLE RUN

Objective: To perform shuttle run as fast as possible. *Testing:* Mark two parallel lines 30 feet apart and place two blocks of wood or similar object behind one of the lines. Students start behind opposite line. On the signal "Ready? Go!" the student runs to the blocks, picks one up, runs back to the starting line, places block behind the line, runs back and picks up the second block, and runs back across starting line. *Rules:* Blocks should not be thrown across the lines. Scores are recorded to the nearest tenth of a second.

ONE MILE RUN/WALK

Objective: To measure heart/lung endurance by fastest time to cover a one-mile distance. *Testing:* On a safe one-mile distance, students begin running on the count "Ready? Go!" Walking may be interspersed with running. However, the students should be encouraged to cover the distance in as short a time as possible. *Rules:* Before administering this test, students' health status should be reviewed. Also, students should be given ample instruction on how to pace themselves and should be allowed to practice running this distance against time. Sufficient time should be allowed for warming up and cooling down before and after the test. Times are recorded in minutes and seconds. *Testing:* Option for 6–7 years old is $1/4$ mile. Option for 8–9 years old is $1/2$ mile. The same objective and testing procedures are used as with the mile run.

PULL-UPS

Objective: To measure upper body strength and endurance by maximum number of pull-ups completed. *Testing:* Student hangs from a horizontal bar at a height the student can hang from with arms fully extended and feet free from floor, using an overhand grasp (palms facing away from body) or underhand grip (palms facing toward the body). Small students may be lifted to starting position. Student raises body until chin clears the bar and then lowers body to full-hang starting position. Student performs as many correct pull-ups as possible. *Rules:* Pull-ups should be done in a smooth rather than jerky motion. Kicking or bending the legs is not permitted and the body must not swing during the movement.

RIGHT-ANGLE PUSH-UPS (OPTION TO PULL-UPS)

Objective: To measure upper body strength/endurance by maximum number of push-ups completed. *Testing:* The student lies face down on the mat in push-up position with hands under shoulders, fingers straight, and legs straight, parallel, and slightly apart, with the toes supporting the feet. The student straightens the arms, keeping the back and knees straight, then lowers the arms until there is a 90-degree angle at the elbows, with the upper arms parallel to the floor. A partner holds her/his hand at the point of the 90-degree angle so that the student being tested goes down only until her/his shoulder touches the partner's hand, then back up. The push-ups are done to a metronome (or audio tape, clapping, drums) with one complete push-up every three seconds, and are continued until the student can do no more in rhythm (has not done the last three in rhythm) or has reached the target number for the PPFA. *Scoring:* Record only those push-ups done with proper form and in rhythm.

FLEXED-ARM HANG

Alternative to pull-ups or right-angle push-ups for National and Participant Physical Fitness Awards. Students who cannot do one pull-up may do the flexed-arm hang in order to qualify for the National or Participant Physical Fitness Awards. To qualify for the Presidential Award, students are required to do pull-ups or the target number of right-angle push-ups. *Objective:* To maintain flexed-arm hang position as long as possible. *Testing:* Using same hand position as in pull-ups, student assumes flexed-arm hang position with chin clearing the bar. Students may be lifted to this position. Student holds this position as long as possible. *Rules:* Chest should be held close to bar with legs hanging straight during hang. Timing is stopped when student's chin touches or falls below the bar.

V-SIT REACH

Objective: To measure flexibility of lower back and hamstrings by reaching forward in the V position. *Testing:* A straight line two feet long is marked on the floor as the baseline. A measuring line is drawn perpendicular to the midpoint of the baseline extending two feet on each side and marked off in half inches. The point where the baseline and measuring line intersect is the "0" point. Student removes shoes and sits on floor with measuring line between legs and soles of feet placed immediately behind baseline, heels 8 to 12 inches apart. Student clasps thumbs so that hands are together palms down, and places them on measuring line. With the legs held flat by a partner, student slowly reaches forward as far as possible, keeping fingers on baseline and feet flexed. After three practice tries, the student holds the fourth reach for three seconds while that distance is recorded. *Rules:* Legs must remain straight with soles of feet held perpendicular to the floor (feet flexed). Student should be encouraged to reach slowly rather than "bounce" while stretching. Scores, recorded to the nearest half inch, are read as plus scores for reaches beyond baseline, minus scores for reaches behind baseline.

SIT AND REACH (OPTION TO THE V-SIT REACH)

Objective: Farthest distance reached. *Testing:* A specially constructed box with a measuring scale marked in centimeters, with 23 centimeters at the level of the feet. Student removes shoes and sits on floor with knees fully extended, feet shoulder-width apart and soles of the feet held flat against the end of the box. With hands on top of each other, palms down, and legs held flat, student reaches along the measuring line as far as possible. After three practice reaches, the fourth reach is held while the distance is recorded. *Rules:* Legs must remain straight, soles of feet against box, and fingertips of both hands should reach evenly along measuring line. Scores are recorded to the nearest centimeter.

90. COMPARISONS OF COMMON FITNESS TESTS

The table below gives you the pros and cons of commonly used tests.

Tests	Advantages	Disadvantages
Height/weight	Simple	Takes no account of muscle mass
Body mass index	Simple	Lacks accuracy
Body fat—calipers	Quick and accurate	Technique needs practice; Interpretation of results
Shuttle run	Large groups can be tested	Accuracy and consistency of measurement
Step test	Simple	Small inaccuracies in measurement of recovery heart rate give large variations in results
Medicine ball throw	Measures arm and upper body strength	Scores influenced by technique
Hand-timed sprints	Easy to administer	Not accurate enough to reflect any changes in performance
Sit and reach	Simple measure	Need to standardize technique

91. BODY MASS INDEX TABLE

Body mass index (BMI) uses a mathematical formula that takes into account both a person's height and weight. BMI equals a person's weight in kilograms divided by height in meters squared (BMI = kg/m^2). To determine BMI, multiply your weight in pounds by 704, then divide by the square of your height in inches. For example, if you weigh 130 pounds and are 5'4" (64") tall, your BMI is (130 × 704) / (64 × 64) = 22.3. (If you use the metric system, divide your weight in kilograms by the square of your height in meters.)

The table below has already done the math and metric conversions. To use the table, find the appropriate height in the left-hand column. Move across the row to the given weight. The number at the top of the column is the BMI for that height and weight.

BMI (kg/m²)	19	20	21	22	23	24	25	26	27	28	29	30	35	40
Height (in.)					**Weight (lb.)**									
58	91	96	100	105	110	115	119	124	129	134	138	143	167	191
59	94	99	104	109	114	119	124	128	133	138	143	148	173	198
60	97	102	107	112	118	123	128	133	138	143	148	153	179	204
61	100	106	111	116	122	127	132	137	143	148	153	158	185	211
62	104	109	115	120	126	131	136	142	147	153	158	164	191	218
63	107	113	118	124	130	135	141	146	152	158	163	169	197	225
64	110	116	122	128	134	140	145	151	157	163	169	174	204	232
65	114	120	126	132	138	144	150	156	162	168	174	180	210	240
66	118	124	130	136	142	148	155	161	167	173	179	186	216	247
67	121	127	134	140	146	153	159	166	172	178	185	191	223	255
68	125	131	138	144	151	158	164	171	177	184	190	197	230	262
69	128	135	142	149	155	162	169	176	182	189	196	203	236	270
70	132	139	146	153	160	167	174	181	188	195	202	207	243	278
71	136	143	150	157	165	172	179	186	193	200	208	215	250	286
72	140	147	154	162	169	177	184	191	199	206	213	221	258	294
73	144	151	159	166	174	182	189	197	204	212	219	227	265	302
74	148	155	163	171	179	186	194	202	210	218	225	233	272	311
75	152	160	168	176	184	192	200	208	216	224	232	240	279	319
76	156	164	172	180	189	197	205	213	221	230	238	246	287	328

Body weight in pounds according to height and body mass index.

Adapted from Bray, G.A., Gray, D.S., Obesity, Part I, Pathogenesis, *West J Med* 1988: 149: 429–441.

92. RISK OF DISEASES ASSOCIATED WITH OBESITY ACCORDING TO BMI

Body mass index, or BMI, is the measurement of choice for many physicians and researchers studying obesity. BMI uses a mathematical formula that takes into account both a person's height and weight. BMI equals a person's weight in kilograms divided by height in meters squared. (BMI = kg/m^2).

BMI	Body Size	Risk of Disease
18.5 or less	Underweight	Not applicable
18.5–24.9	Normal	Not applicable
25.0–29.9	Overweight	Increased, High
30.0–34.9	Obese	High, Very high
35.0–39.9	Obese	Very high
40 or greater	Extremely Obese	Extremely high

93. GENERAL GUIDELINES FOR CHILDREN'S WEIGHT

4 years

average weight = 37 male/35 female

lower limit = 31 male/30 female

upper limit = 43 male/41.7 female

6 years

average weight = 45 male/44 female

lower limit = 38 male/37 female

upper limit = 53 male/53 female

8 years

average weight = 55 male/55 female

lower limit = 48 male/45 female

upper limit = 68 male/70 female

10 years

average weight = 68 male/71 female

lower limit = 56 male/57 female

upper limit = 90 male/98 female

12 years

average weight = 88 male/92 female

lower limit = 70 male/72 female

upper limit = 112 male/123 female

14 years

average weight = 112 male/110 female

lower limit = 90 male/90 female

upper limit = 145 male/145 female

16 years

average weight = 136 male/123 female

lower limit = 112 male/100 female

upper limit = 172 male/158 female

18 years

average weight =152 male/124 female

lower limit = 127 male/105 female

upper limit = 195 male/160 female

94. HARVARD STEP TEST

The objective of this test is to monitor the development of the athlete's cardiovascular system.

➟ **Procedure:** The athlete steps up and down on the platform at a rate of 30 steps per minute for 5 minutes or until exhaustion. Exhaustion is defined as when the athlete cannot maintain the stepping rate for 15 seconds. The athlete immediately sits down on completion of the test, and the heartbeats are counted for 1 to 1.5 (1st pulse count), 2 to 2.5 (2nd pulse count), and 3 to 3.5 (3rd pulse count) minutes.

➟ **Equipment required:** Step or platform 20 inches (50.8 cm) high, stopwatch, metronome or cadence tape.

➟ **Scoring:** The score is equal to (100 × test duration in seconds) divided by 2 × (total heartbeats in the recovery periods).

- excellent   > 90
- good   80–89
- high average   65–79
- low average   55–64
- poor   < 55

95. HARVARD STEP TEST RESULTS SHEET

1. Time of Exercise: Seconds _____ × 100 = _____
2. 1st pulse count (A)   _____
   2nd pulse count (B)   _____
   3rd pulse count (C)   _____
   Add A, B, C to get total: _____ × 2 = _____
3. Divide the total of #1 by the total of #2 to get a total of _____.
4. The total of #3 indicates a Harvard Step Test Score of _____.
5. The score indicates a cardiovascular rating that is _____.

Score	Cardiovascular Rating
> 90	Excellent
80–89	Good
65–79	High average
55–64	Low average
< 55	Poor

96. HISTORICAL FACTS ABOUT FLAG AND TOUCH FOOTBALL

➡ "Touch football" is entered in *Webster's Dictionary*, 1933.

➡ "Flag football" is entered in *Webster's Dictionary*, 1954.

➡ Flag football is believed to have begun in the U.S. military during World War II to prevent injury to military personnel playing football.

➡ Fort Meade in Maryland has the first recorded history of flag football and is generally accepted as its birthplace.

➡ Local leagues were formed as military personnel returned home in the 1950s and 1960s.

97. FLAG AND TOUCH FOOTBALL EQUIPMENT

Ball: A regulation leather or rubber-coated football can be used. It is generally recommended that a smaller sized football be used for younger children.

Flags: Flags should measure 12 to 15 inches in length and 2 inches in width. They can be made of plastic or cloth and can be tucked in the top of the gym pant if belts are not available.

Goals: Although goal posts are not necessary, extra points must be run in after a touchdown if goal posts are not available. Cones may be used as goals.

98. FLAG AND TOUCH FOOTBALL PLAYING FIELD

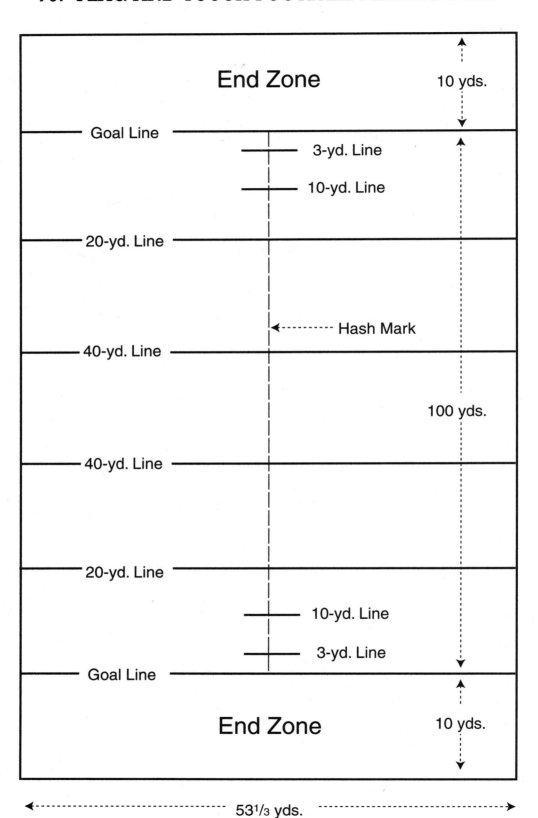

End Zone — 10 yds.

Goal Line

3-yd. Line

10-yd. Line

20-yd. Line

Hash Mark

40-yd. Line

100 yds.

40-yd. Line

20-yd. Line

10-yd. Line

3-yd. Line

Goal Line

End Zone — 10 yds.

53⅓ yds.

99. FLAG AND TOUCH FOOTBALL RULES

The game allows players to participate in a relatively safe situation while still retaining many of the skills used in football. The rules for touch football and flag football are generally the same. However, when playing flag football, the rules for blocking, fumbling, and tackling must be strictly enforced. In flag football, any ball carrier without two flags is considered tackled. In order to minimize hazardous play, the following precautionary measures are suggested:

➡ No blocking, tackling, or holding the ball carrier.

➡ Defensive players must maintain contact with the ground.

➡ Ball carriers may not employ straight-arm or body contact.

Length of Game

➡ Four 10- to 12-minute periods constitute a game with a 1-minute rest between periods and a 5-minute rest between halves.

Players

➡ A team generally consists of seven players, and the offensive team must have at least three players on the line of scrimmage when the ball is put into play. Any number of substitutions may be made at any time during a stoppage of play.

Overtime

Tie games may be decided by one of the following methods:

➡ Award the game to the team with the greater number of penetrations inside the opponent's 20-yard line.

➡ Award the game to the team with the greater number of first downs.

➡ Give each team four downs from the 20-yard line and award the game to the team advancing the ball farther.

Timeouts

➡ Each team is allowed two timeouts per half. Timeouts are taken:

- When the ball goes out of bounds
- After a score is made
- While a penalty is being enforced
- At the direction of the referee
- At the end of each period

Scoring

➡ Scoring is the same as regulation football:

- Touchdown = 6 points
- Field Goal = 3 points
- Safety = 2 points
- Kick after touchdown = 1 point (2 points by run or pass)

100. FLAG AND TOUCH FOOTBALL PLAYING REGULATIONS

Putting the Ball in Play

➤ The ball is put into play by a place kick from the kicker's 20-yard line at the start of the game, after a score, and at the beginning of the third quarter.

➤ Defensive players must be 10 yards away when the ball is kicked.

➤ Members of the kicking team must be behind the ball.

➤ The ball must travel 10 yards or be rekicked.

➤ If the ball goes out of bounds after 10 yards, the opponent has the choice of beginning play where it went out of bounds or placing it on his or her own 20-yard line.

➤ If the ball is kicked into the end zone and the opponents choose not to run it back, play begins on their 20-yard line.

Fumbled Ball

➤ A fumbled ball at any time is considered a dead ball and belongs to the team that committed the fumble.

➤ The down and point to be gained remains the same.

➤ A fumbled forward pass is ruled as an incomplete pass.

Downed Ball

➤ In touch football, the ball is dead or the player is downed when an opponent touches him or her with one hand between the shoulders and knees.

➤ In flag football, the ball is downed or the player is tackled when one flag is detached from the belt or the ball carrier loses his or her flag.

First Downs

➤ Each team has four chances to move the ball from one 20-yard zone to the next.

➤ If a team is not successful at moving the ball from one zone to the next in four downs, the ball is awarded to the opponents on the spot where the last stoppage of play occurred.

Passing

➤ All players on both teams are eligible to catch passes.

➤ Forward passes may be thrown from any point back of the line of scrimmage.

➤ Lateral passes may be thrown anywhere on the field.

➤ Any number of passes may be thrown in a series of downs.

101. FLAG AND TOUCH FOOTBALL PENALTIES

5-Yard Penalty Infractions (Taken from Line of Scrimmage)

➡ Offside

➡ Delay of game

➡ Less than three players on the line of scrimmage

➡ Illegal motion

➡ Illegal forward pass

15-Yard Penalty Infractions (Taken from Spot of Foul)

➡ Illegal use of hands

➡ Illegal block

➡ Unnecessary roughness: pushing, tackling, shoving, tripping, holding

➡ Unsportsmanlike conduct

➡ Clipping

➡ Pass interference

Flagrant rule violations result in ejection from game.

102. FLAG AND TOUCH FOOTBALL TERMS*

Backs — Players on the team who are stationed behind the linemen and who ordinarily carry or pass the ball on offense.

Block — Action of offensive linemen and backs in which they use their bodies to ward off defensive players from the ball carrier.

Button hook — A forward pass play in which the receiver runs toward the defender, turns, and runs back toward the passer to receive the pass.

Clipping — A blocking action in which a player throws his or her body across the back of the leg(s) of a player not carrying the ball. This can cause injury and is a personal foul.

Cut-back — An offensive maneuver in which the back starts wide and then cuts back toward center of the line.

Fair catch — A player may make a fair catch on a kickoff, return kick, or kick from scrimmage by raising a hand clearly above his or her head before making the catch. He or she may not be tackled or take more than two steps after receiving the ball.

Flanker — An offensive maneuver in which a player lines up nearer the sideline than a designated opponent.

Forward pass — An offensive play in which the ball is thrown toward the line of scrimmage.

Handoff — An offensive play in which one back hands off the ball to another back who attempts to advance the ball.

Lateral pass — An offensive play in which the ball is passed sideward or backward to the line of scrimmage.

Line of scrimmage — An imaginary line, or vertical plane, passing through the end of the ball nearer a team's goal line and parallel to the goal lines. There is a line of scrimmage for each team, and the area between the two lines is called the *neutral zone*. Any player of either team is offside if he or she encroaches upon the neutral zone before the ball is snapped.

Neutral zone — The imaginary line that passes between the lines of scrimmage for each team. Either team is offside if it moves across the neutral zone before the ball is snapped.

Offside — When an offensive player is ahead of the ball before it is snapped. (The penalty is five yards.)

Safety — A score made when a free ball, or one in possession of a player defending his or her own goal, becomes dead behind the goal, provided the impetus that caused it to cross the goal was supplied by the defending team.

Screen pass   An offensive maneuver in which a wave of eligible receivers converge in the area where a pass is to be thrown.

Shotgun offense   A formation in which the quarterback lines up five to six yards behind the center. Usually one or both halfbacks may line up one to two yards on either side of the quarterback and one yard in front of the quarterback.

Shovel pass   An offensive maneuver in which a pass is thrown, underhand, usually forward to a back behind the line of scrimmage.

Touchback   When a ball that is legally in possession of a player guarding his own goal becomes dead behind the opponent's goal line, provided the impetus that caused it to cross the goal line was supplied by an opponent. No points are scored on the play, and the ball is put in play at the 20-yard line.

---

*American Association for Health, Physical Education, and Recreation, *Rules for Coeducational Activities and Sports.* Revised ed. Washington, DC: AAHPER Publications, 1980.

103. FLOOR HOCKEY FACTS

➡ Tom Harter, director of Civic Recreation in Battle Creek, Michigan, developed floor hockey in 1962.

➡ There are only four general playing rules, so the game can be learned quickly.

➡ The game is designed for strenuous activity and continuous play.

➡ The game combines the rules of ice hockey and basketball.

➡ Emphasis is placed on playing the puck, not the opponent.

➡ Body checking is absolutely forbidden, making it safe and ideal as a coed activity.

104. FLOOR HOCKEY PLAYING AREA

➡ Any gymnasium that is laid out for basketball can be used.

➡ The *center line* is the mid-court line of a basketball court.

➡ The *center circle* is the basketball mid-court jump circle. Play always begins in this circle to start the game, after a goal, or after a penalty.

➡ *Goals* are any marked area not to exceed 58 by 46 inches. Hockey nets are recommended, although cones are commonly used.

➡ The *goal box* is a line 5 feet from the front of the goal and 4 feet on each side of the goal.

105. FLOOR HOCKEY POSITIONS

Each team consists of 6 player positions:

➡ A *goalkeeper* who may stop shots with hands, feet, or stick.

➡ A *center*, who is the only player allowed to move full court and who leads offensive play. The center usually has his or her stick striped with black tape.

➡ Two *defensive players* who may not go past the center line into the offensive area and whose responsibility is to keep the puck out of the defensive end of the court.

➡ Two *forwards* who may not go past the center line into the defensive area and who work with the center setting up offensive plays.

106. BASIC RULES OF FLOOR HOCKEY

The Game

➡ The game consists of three periods of 8 minutes each with 5 minutes between periods.

➡ The first period starts with a flip for possession.

➡ The team that is behind in the scoring after the first and second periods is given possession of the puck to start play in the second and third periods.

➡ Play starts on the whistle.

➡ Penalty for starting before the whistle is loss of possession.

➡ The center must have one foot inside of the circle and start play with a pass from the circle.

➡ All other players must be outside of the 10-foot restraining circle.

➡ Goals may not be scored directly off the pass from the center circle on the start of play.

The Play

➡ Time starts when the ball is put into play by the center and is touched by a member of either team.

➡ The clock will stop when a goal is scored or a roughing foul or misconduct is called. Play is not stopped for running fouls.

➡ Free substitution is permitted at any time.

➡ Change of positions between guards and forwards may be made only when the puck is dead, a goal is scored, or a roughing or misconduct foul is called.

➡ There is no out-of-bounds.

➡ There are no team timeouts.

➡ Overtime games are "sudden death" (first goal scored) with each period being 5 minutes with a 2-minute rest period between periods.

Scoring

➡ One point is scored each time the puck passes across the goal line.

➡ If the puck crosses the goal line while in the air, it must hit the back wall of the goal to count for a score.

➡ Pucks can deflect off of a player or equipment.

➡ Pucks cannot be kicked into the goal.

➡ Goals do not score on a foul.

Goalkeeping

➡ The goalkeeper must wear a mask.

➡ It is recommended that the goalkeeper wear hockey shin pads and stomach protector.

➡ It is recommended that the goalkeeper wear a ball glove on his or her catching hand.

➡ The goalkeeper must use his or her hands to clear the puck away from the goal.

➡ The goalkeeper may not hold or throw the puck towards the other end of the playing area.

➡ The penalty for throwing the puck is loss of possession and a misconduct foul.

➡ No other player may enter the goal box without being charged with misconduct.

➡ The goalkeeper will be charged with misconduct if he or she holds the puck for more than three seconds.

➡ The goalkeeper may be pulled from the goal box, but is restricted to the center line.

107. FLOOR HOCKEY FOULS

Players charged with a running foul, roughing foul, or misconduct must sit out two minutes. His or her team must play shorthanded for this period. If the opposition during the penalty scores a goal, the player may return to the floor.

Running Fouls

➡ Defense players and forwards crossing over center line.

➡ Touching the puck with the hand.

➡ Swinging the stick above waist height.

➡ Goalie throwing the puck.

➡ Player other than goalie entering the goal box.

➡ Chopping at the puck to raise it in the air (with the exception of a shot on goal).

Roughing Fouls

➡ Hacking or striking with the stick.

➡ Pushing.

➡ Tripping.

➡ Blocking with the body.

➡ Any action considered dangerous to other players.

➡ High sticking above the shoulders.

➡ Slashing with the stick (with or without contact to another player).

Misconduct Fouls

➡ Any time play is deliberately stopped by lying on, stepping on, or holding puck.

➡ Too many players on the floor.

➡ Offensive or defensive players (other than goalie) in goal box area with their stick.

108. FLOOR TENNIS FACTS

➡ Floor tennis is a combination of tennis and ping-pong.

➡ Floor tennis is a lead-up game to many racket sports, pickleball being one of them.

➡ The game can be played with doubles or singles.

➡ Ping-pong paddles and a ping-pong ball are used.

➡ The game is played on an 8 by 16-foot court.

➡ A 2 by 8-foot board or net can be used.

➡ Hand/eye coordination and teamwork are very important in floor tennis.

➡ Floor tennis involves strategies with both players working as a team.

➡ The players may be anywhere on the court, but the ball must bounce once before it can be hit.

➡ Rushing the net is *not* a good strategy in floor tennis.

109. FLOOR TENNIS EQUIPMENT

➡ Four ping-pong paddles per court.

➡ One ping-pong ball per court.

➡ One 2′ by 4′ by $1/4$″ net made of plywood, wood, netting, or any appropriate material.

110. FLOOR TENNIS ETIQUETTE

➡ Be honest.

➡ Be a good sport.

➡ *Discuss*, do not argue.

➡ *Walk* from court to court when rotating.

➡ Do not touch or reach over the net at any time.

➡ If your ball enters another court, do not interfere with that game. Wait for a stoppage of play to retrieve the ball.

111. FLOOR TENNIS COURT

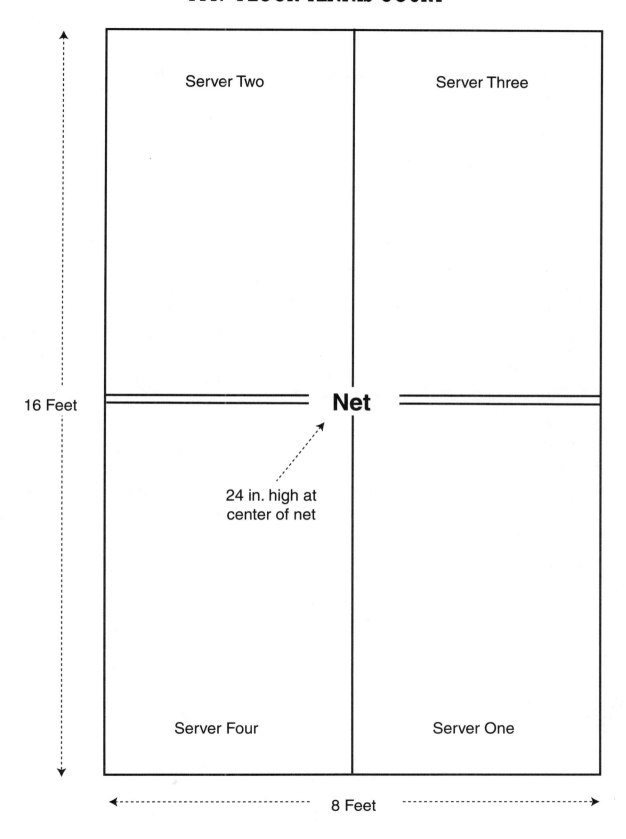

112. BASIC RULES OF FLOOR TENNIS

➡ Play begins with selected server *bouncing* the ball once and hitting it over the net diagonally to the cross-court.

➡ The ball is hit with an underhand swing and the server should have one foot behind the baseline.

➡ A serve that hits the top of the net and goes over into the appropriate court is reserved.

➡ Serve rotates every two points.

➡ The rotation goes back and forth between players until each has served two points.

➡ Server *must always* say or call the score before serving.

➡ The ball *must* bounce once on your side of the court before it may be returned.

➡ After the serve is made, the ball may be returned to either of the opponent's courts and may be played by either opponent *after* it bounces once.

➡ A ball that strikes a player in the air is considered in and a point for the other team.

➡ A ball that hits on the line is a good ball and should be returned. Lines are in play. A line call is made by the team on that side.

➡ Once the ball is in play, all balls that hit the net and land across the net in bounds are considered fair and must be returned.

➡ A point is scored when an opponent fails to return any shot that lands in his or her court.

➡ Play continues until time is called (5-minute games).

➡ When time is called, all play must stop, and paddles are returned to the baseline position.

➡ Points being played when time is called are not counted.

➡ Tie games are decided by a 1-point playoff game.

113. BASIC FOUR SQUARE (BOX BALL) RULES

The Game

➡ The game requires a flat, hard surface and a large rubber ball, soccer ball, or basketball.

➡ The game is played in a square court subdivided into four equal-size playing squares.

➡ Although any size court is acceptable, 6 to 8 feet per square is recommended.

➡ Each square should be labeled A, B, C, D (or 1, 2, 3, 4).

➡ The object of the game is to advance sequentially from the A (or 1) square to the D (or 4) square and stay there for as many turns as possible.

The Serve

➡ The ball must be hit from behind the diagonal line.

➡ The player must remain behind the line until the ball bounces in another box.

➡ The ball must be hit with two hands, little fingers touching, and underside of the ball.

➡ The ball must be hit in front of the player's body.

➡ The ball must bounce in another player's box.

➡ The ball must be served between the knees and the head of the receiving player.

➡ The person standing in the highest lettered (or numbered) square always serves.

➡ In a successful serve, the server drops the ball in his or her own square, lets it bounce once, and then hits it into another square.

➡ If the person to whom the ball was served lets it bounce in his or her own square once then hits it into another square, the serve is complete and play continues.

➡ If he or she actually touched the ball but did not cause it to land legally in an opponent's square, he or she is out.

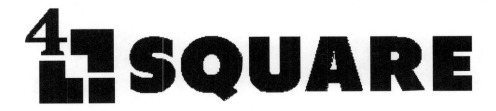

The Volley

→ After a successful serve, play continues with volleying from one square to another.

→ If a player fails to volley legally, he or she is out.

→ In a legal volley, the ball bounces only once in a player's square, then continues to an opponent's square.

→ The player can hit the ball before it bounces in his or her square to gain control of it.

→ Whether or not the person hits the ball before it bounces, he or she must hit the ball once after it bounces.

→ Any instantaneous touch of the ball is considered a hit.

→ If the ball bounces out of bounds (out of the court) or on a boundary line, the last person to touch it is out.

→ If a ball hits a player without bouncing first, it is considered out if the player is outside a square, and in play if the player is in a square.

Fouls

→ Any player who commits a foul is out.

→ A *bobble* occurs when a player hits the ball more than once between bounces.

→ If a player touches the ball only once, but his or her hand remains in contact with the ball longer than the instantaneous time of a hit, the player is said to have *carried* the ball.

→ Touching the ball with two hands, unless both hands hit simultaneously, is considered *holding*.

→ Any hit that causes the ball to bounce up higher than the head of the receiver is a *slam*.

Rotation

→ When a player gets out, the person loses his or her position on the court. If there are no more players than there are spaces, the person who is out moves to the A (or 1) spot. If there are more players than squares, the person who is out gets in line. The first and second players waiting in line become judges. Players in squares lettered (or numbered) lower than this person's original square advance to the next higher letter (or number) square.

114. FOUR SQUARE (BOX BALL) COURT

2	1
3	4

115. FOUR SQUARE (BOX BALL) STRATEGIES

➡ The best-placed balls are the ones that cannot be returned.

➡ Place the ball in a corner far from the player.

➡ Balls that bounce deep in the corners are very hard to be returned.

➡ Some players play too far forward. Place the ball near the outside line.

➡ Some players play too far back. Place the ball near the inside line.

➡ Each player should send the ball to a player in a higher letter (or number) box and all players should try to get the server out:

  • Player 1 tries to get out 2, 3, and server.

  • Player 2 tries to get out 3 and server.

  • Player 3 tries to get out the server.

116. FOUR SQUARE (BOX BALL) GAMES

Bobbling	You may hit the ball as many times as you like.
Chicken Leg	You can hit the ball with any part of your body.
Double Taps	You may hit the ball as many as two times or *only* two times.
Isolation	When isolation is declared in a certain square, anyone who hits the ball to that square is out.
Quadruple Taps	You may hit the ball as many as four times or *only* four times.
Triple Taps	You may hit the ball as many as three times or *only* three times.

117. HISTORICAL FACTS ABOUT FRISBEE™

➡ **1920**   Yale students discover the sport of throwing pie tins from the Mother Frisbie's Baking Company of Bridgeport, Connecticut.

➡ **1948**   The first plastic flying disc is manufactured by Fred Morrison, a California carpenter and building inspector.

➡ **1957**   The WHAM-O company introduces a flying plastic disc called the Pluto Platter.

➡ **1958**   WHAM-O modifies its plastic flying disc, trademarks the name Frisbee, and renames the Pluto Platter.

➡ **1958**   First International Frisbee™ Tournament is held in Escanaba, Michigan.

➡ **1967**   The International Frisbee™ Association is founded.

➡ **1968**   The U.S. Navy spends nearly $400,000 to test Frisbee™ discs as vehicles for keeping flares aloft.

➡ **1969**   Ultimate is invented in Maplewood, New Jersey by Columbia High School students.

➡ **1973**   The first intercollegiate Ultimate game is played between Rutgers University and Princeton University in New Jersey.

➡ **1973**   The first all-dog flying disc competition is held at California State University, Fullerton.

➡ **1973**   The World Frisbee™ Disc Championships are held in the Rose Bowl, Pasadena, California.

➡ **1979**   A gentleman by the name of Tom Kennedy wins a $50,000 disc golf tournament in Huntington Beach, California.

➡ **1986**   Cub Scouts introduce an activity badge for participation in Ultimate.

➡ **1993**   The President's Council on Physical Fitness and Sports accepts flying disc sports as a new category for the Presidential Sports Award.

118. FRISBEE™ GAMES

Guts

→ Played between two teams of one to five players each.

→ The objective is to be the first team to score 21 points.

→ To start play, each team lines up facing each other 14 meters apart.

→ Players attempt to throw the disc toward or at the opposing team, and within the reach of that team, in such a manner that the opposing team cannot make a clean catch.

→ A good throw, without a catch, results in 1 point for the throwing team and a bad throw results in 1 point for the receiving team.

→ A good throw is made when the throw travels to or through the scoring zone of a player on the receiving team without first touching the ground.

→ In order to be considered a clean catch, the disc:

  • Must be held in *one* hand long enough to establish complete control.

  • May not be touched by any two parts of a player's body at any one time.

  • May not touch the ground before it is caught.

→ A point is scored by the throwing team whenever a good throw is made into a scoring zone of one of the receiving players and the receiving team fails to make a good catch.

→ The receiving team scores a point whenever the throwing team fails to make a good throw.

→ The receiving team is not required to make a good catch if a good throw is not made.

→ A good throw by the throwing team with a corresponding good catch by the receiving team will not be scored as a point for either team.

Ultimate

→ Combines elements of soccer, football, and touch football.

→ The goal is for the team with the disc to pass it up the field without dropping it and catch it in the end zone.

→ The other team tries to intercept the disc or knock it down.

→ A regulation game has seven players on each team.

→ A regulation field is 70 by 40 yards, with 25-yard end zones.

→ Each point begins with both teams lining up on the front of their respective end zone.

→ The defense throws the disc to the offense.

→ Each time the offense completes a pass in the defense's end zone, the offense scores a point.

→ The disc may be advanced in any direction by completing a pass to a teammate.

→ Players may not run with the disc.

→ The player with the disc has ten seconds to throw the disc.

→ When a pass is not completed, the defense immediately takes possession of the disc and becomes the offense.

→ Substitutions may be made after a score and during an injury timeout.

→ No physical contact is allowed between players.

→ Picks and screens are also prohibited.

→ Contact with another player is a foul.

→ When a foul disrupts possession, the play resumes as if the possession was retained.

→ Ultimate stresses sportsmanship and fair play.

Disc Golf

→ The game consists of throwing a disc from a teeing area to a target by a throw or successive throws.

→ The competitor who plays the stipulated round or rounds in the fewest throws (including penalty throws) is the winner.

→ Players should not throw until they are certain that the thrown disc will not distract another player or potentially injure anyone present.

→ Players should watch the other members of their group throw in order to aid in locating errant throws and to ensure compliance with the rules.

→ Players should take care not to produce any distracting noises or any potential visual distractions for other players who are throwing.

→ Discourteous actions include shouting, freestyling, throwing out of turn, throwing or kicking equipment, and advancing on the fairway before the other players have thrown.

→ Teeing order on the first teeing area is determined by the order in which the scorecards were filled out or by the order the players were listed or arranged on the scoreboard.

→ The scores on the previous hole, with the lowest score throwing first, etc., determine teeing order on all subsequent tees.

→ If the previous hole was a tie, the scores are to be counted back until the order is resolved.

→ After all the players in the group have teed off, the player farthest from the hole (the away player) throws first.

119. BASIC FRISBEE™ (FLYING DISC) THROWS

Basic Backhand Throw

➡ Right handers: Stand with the right shoulder facing the target.

➡ Left handers: Stand with the left shoulder facing the target.

➡ Spread the feet about hip-width apart, with knees flexed slightly.

➡ Grip the edge of the disc firmly, but not tightly.

➡ Place the thumb on top, with the first two or three fingers underneath and slightly behind.

➡ Bring the arm backwards, so that the disc is next to the rear leg and the body's weight is shifted slightly back.

➡ Drop the forearm a bit below parallel, so that the disc is at a 45-degree angle.

➡ Bring the arm forward with smooth, controlled force.

➡ Keep the disc at an angle to the ground.

➡ As the arm is brought forward, shift the body's weight forward and step the front foot ahead slightly. The point in the motion at which the disc is released will determine where it goes.

➡ As the disc is released, snap the wrist forward, so that the disc "jumps" off the side of the first finger. This will give spin to the disc and stabilize it in flight.

➡ The harder the wrist is snapped, the more spin the disc gains and the better the throw will be.

➡ Keep the wrist in line with the arm as it's snapped.

➡ Continue the arm motion (follow through) to help direct the disc towards its target.

Basic Sidearm Throw

➡ Right handers: Stand with the left shoulder forward and torso turned slightly towards the target.

➡ Left handers: Stand with the right shoulder forward and torso turned slightly towards the target.

➡ Keep feet shoulder-width apart.

➡ Keep the arm behind the rear leg and flex knees.

➡ Grip the edge of the disc firmly.

➡ Place thumb on top, and the first two or three fingers underneath and slightly behind.

➡ Bring the arm backwards, so that the disc is next to the rear leg.

➡ Shift the weight slightly back.

➡ Drop the forearm a bit below parallel, so that the disc is at about a 45-degree angle.

➡ Most of the force comes from the wrist snap and weight transfer, since the arm only moves a short distance.

➡ Bring the arm forward with considerable force.

➡ The elbow will be the pivot point, and the hand will actually stop with a jerk before it reaches the front leg.

➡ As the arm is brought forward, step the foot facing the target forward a bit as the weight shifts forward. The importance of the release point and wrist snap are magnified with this throw.

➡ As the arm only travels a short distance, the possible release points are much closer together. Even a slight variance will greatly affect the flight direction.

➡ A good starting point is to release the disc just after the wrist crosses the rear leg. The disc angle must be fairly steep when released.

➡ Snap the wrist quite firmly on the release.

➡ This throw will not be successful unless the disc has good spin.

➡ After the disc leaves the hand, keep the first two fingers firmly extended.

➡ Following through is not necessary or desirable in this throw.

120. HISTORICAL FACTS ABOUT GOLF

→ Although the actual origins of golf are unknown, there is evidence that the game began in St. Andrews, Scotland, before the founding of the University in 1411.

→ King James II of Scotland felt that golf was interfering with archery practice, so he banned the game by a Scottish Act of Parliament in 1457.

→ In many parts of Scotland's East Coast, parishioners were punished for playing golf on the Sabbath.

→ Interest in golf later expanded to England.

→ Mary Queen of Scots lost a match to one of her attendants, Mary Seton, and presented her with a famous necklace.

→ Mary Queen of Scots was reprimanded for playing golf at Seton House shortly after the murder of her husband, Lord Darnley, in 1567.

→ In the first known reference to golf in America, golf was banned from the streets of Albany, New York in 1659.

→ The Company of Gentlemen Golfers was established in Edinburgh, at Leith Links, in 1744, and introduced the first set of rules.

→ The United States Golf Association (USGA) and the Royal and Ancient Golf Club of St. Andrews currently govern the rules of golf.

→ The USGA governs play in the United States.

→ The Professionals Championship was opened to amateurs in 1861, and the British Open was born.

→ St. Andrews, one of the oldest golf clubs in the United States, was established as a 3-hole layout in 1888 at Yonkers, New York. It was extended to 6 holes on a cow pasture.

→ The first 18-hole course in the United States, the Chicago Golf Club, was founded near Wheaton, Illinois in 1893.

→ There were 387 golf courses worldwide in 1890.

→ The number had grown to 1,280 by 1895.

→ It had taken 500 years to build the first 400 courses, and just 5 more years to triple that number.

→ There were 80 courses in the U.S. in 1896.

→ Almost 6,000 courses had been built by 1930.

121. GENTLEMEN GOLFERS OF LEITH 1744—RULES OF GOLF

1. You must Tee your Ball within a Club length of the Hole.

2. Your Tee must be upon the ground.

3. You are not to change the Ball which you strike off the Tee.

4. You are not to remove Stones, Bones, or any Break-club for the sake of playing your Ball, except upon the fair Green, and that only within a Club length of your Ball.

5. If your Ball come among Water, or any watery filth, you are at liberty to take out your Ball, and bringing it behind the hazard, and teeing it, you may play it with any club and allow your Adversary a stroke for so getting out your Ball.

6. If your Balls be found anywhere touching one another, you are to lift the first Ball till you play the last.

7. At holing, you are to play your Ball honestly for the Hole, and not play upon your Adversary's Ball, not lying in your way to the Hole.

8. If you should lose your Ball by its being taken up, or in any other way, you are to go back to the spot where you struck last, and drop another Ball, and allow your Adversary a stroke for your misfortune.

9. No man, at Holing his Ball, is to be allowed to mark to the Hole with his Club or anything else.

10. If a Ball be stop'd by any person, Horse, Dog, or anything else, the Ball so stop'd must be played where it lyes.

11. If you draw your Club in order to strike, and proceed as far in the stroke as to be bringing down your Club—if then your Club shall break in any way, it is to be accounted a stroke.

12. He whose Ball lyes farthest from the Hole is obliged to play first.

13. Neither Trench, Ditch, nor Dyke made for the preservation of the Links, nor the Scholars' holes, nor the Soldiers' lines, shall be accounted a Hazard, but the Ball is to be taken out, Teed, and played with any iron Club.

122. BASIC RULES OF GOLF

Golf is a game in which a ball is struck with a club from a prepared area, known as the *tee*, across *fairway* and *rough* to a second prepared area, which has a hole in it, known as the *putting green*. The object of the game is to complete what is known as a *hole* by playing a ball from the tee into the hole on the putting green in the fewest possible number of strokes. A round of golf consists of playing 18 holes. There are two forms of play: *match play* which is decided by holes won and lost, and *stroke play* which is decided by the total number of strokes taken to complete the round. You are allowed a maximum of 14 clubs to play a round.

Teeing Off

➡ Tee off between, and up to two club-lengths behind, the front line of the tee markers.

➡ There is no penalty in match play for teeing off outside this area, but an opponent may ask for a replay of the stroke.

➡ A two-stroke penalty is incurred in stroke play and play continues from within the proper area.

Playing the Ball

➡ The ball must be played where it lies.

➡ The lie, the area of the intended swing or the line of play, may not be improved by moving, bending, or breaking anything fixed or growing except in taking a stance or making the swing.

➡ If the ball lies in a bunker or a water hazard, the ground in the bunker or the ground or water in the water hazard may not be touched, before the downswing.

➡ If a wrong ball is played in match play, the hole is lost.

➡ If a wrong ball is played in stroke play, a two-stroke penalty is incurred and the correct ball must then be played.

On the Putting Green

➡ Ball marks and old hole plugs on the line of the putt may be repaired, but not spike marks or any other damage.

➡ A ball may be marked, lifted, and cleaned on the putting green, but it must be replaced on the exact spot.

➡ The putting surface may not be tested by scraping it or rolling a ball over it.

➡ If a ball played from the putting green strikes the flagstick in match play, the hole is lost.

➡ In stroke play, a two-stroke penalty is incurred.

Moving a Ball at Rest

➡ If the ball is at rest and it is moved by the player, or if it moves after the player has addressed it, a penalty stroke is added and the ball is replaced.

➡ If the ball is at rest and is moved by someone else or another ball, it is replaced with no penalty.

Deflecting or Stopping a Ball in Motion

➡ If the ball struck by the player is deflected or stopped by the player in match play, the hole is lost.

➡ In stroke play, a two-stroke penalty is incurred and the ball is played as it lies.

➡ If a ball struck by a player is deflected or stopped by someone else, the ball is played as it lies without penalty.

➡ If the ball struck by a player is deflected or stopped by another ball at rest in match play, no penalty is incurred and the ball is played as it lies.

➡ In stroke play, a two-stroke penalty is incurred if both balls were on the putting green before you played.

Lifting, Dropping, and Placing a Ball

➡ If a lifted ball is to be replaced, its position must be marked.

➡ If a ball is to be dropped or placed in any other position, it is recommended that the ball's original position be marked.

➡ When dropping, stand erect, hold the ball at shoulder height and arm's length and drop it.

Loose Impediments

➡ A loose impediment may be moved unless it and the ball are in a hazard.

➡ If a loose impediment is touched within one club-length of the ball and the ball moves, the ball must be replaced and (unless the ball was on the putting green) a penalty stroke is incurred.

Obstructions

➡ Movable obstructions (rakes, etc.) anywhere on the course may be moved and, if the ball moves, it must be replaced without penalty.

➡ If an immovable obstruction (water fountain, etc.) interferes with the player's stance or swing, the ball may be dropped within one club-length of the nearest point of relief not nearer the hole.

Casual Water, Ground Under Repair, Etc.

➡ If the ball is in casual water, ground under repair, or a hole made by a burrowing animal, the ball may be dropped without penalty within one club-length of the nearest point of relief not nearer the hole.

Water Hazards

➡ If the ball lies in a water hazard, play the ball as it lies or, under penalty of one stroke:

- Drop any distance behind the water hazard keeping a straight line between the hole, the point where the ball crossed the margin of the water hazard and spot on which the ball is dropped.
- Play again from where the ball was hit into the hazard.

➡ If the ball is in a lateral water hazard, in addition to the options for a ball in a water hazard, under penalty of one stroke, the ball may be dropped within two club-lengths of:

- The point where the ball crossed the margin of the hazard.
- A point on the opposite side of the hazard no closer to the hole.

Ball Lost or Out of Bounds

➡ If the ball is lost outside a water hazard or out of bounds, another ball must be played from the spot where the last shot was played under penalty of one stroke.

➡ Five minutes are permitted to search for a ball, after which if it is not found it is considered lost.

➡ A *provisional ball* may be played if a player thinks the ball is lost outside a water hazard or out of bounds.

➡ It must be stated that it is a provisional ball and it must be hit before the player goes forward to search for the original ball.

➡ If the original ball is lost or out of bounds, the player must continue with the provisional ball under penalty of one stroke.

➡ If the original ball is not lost or out of bounds, the player must continue play of the hole with the original ball and the provisional ball must be abandoned.

Ball Unplayable

➡ If a player believes the ball is unplayable outside a water hazard, under penalty of one stroke, a player may:

- Drop within two club-lengths of where the ball lies not nearer the hole.
- Drop any distance behind the point where the ball lay keeping a straight line between the hole, the point where the ball lay and the spot on which the ball is dropped.
- Replay the shot.

123. GOLF RULES OF ETIQUETTE

Etiquette includes courtesy on the course and care of the course. The following rules of etiquette are not rules that incur any penalty, but they are an important part of the game of golf.

1. Don't move, talk, or stand close to any player during his or her swing.
2. Don't play until the group in front is out of the way.
3. Always play without delay. Leave the putting green as soon as all players in your group have holed out.
4. Invite faster groups to play through.
5. Replace divots. Smooth footprints in bunkers.
6. Don't step on the line of another player's putt.
7. Don't drop clubs on the putting green.
8. Replace the flagstick carefully.

124. GOLF CLUBS

The Clubs

➡ A set of clubs consists of 14 clubs (woods, irons, and a putter).

➡ The higher the number of the club, the shorter the club's length and the more sharply angled the club face (which gives the club a greater degree of loft).

➡ Grips, shaft material, hosels, and club head material all affect the balance point (swing weight) of the club and can affect a golfer's ability to make a shot.

➡ Grips are generally made of leather or synthetic material and should be chosen on the basis of comfort.

➡ Shafts can be made of steel or graphite composite material and vary in flexibility.

➡ A stiff shaft should be used by the stronger players and a more flexible club should be used by golfers of lesser strength.

CLUB SPECIFICATIONS

The loft of the club increases by 4 degrees and the shaft decreases by $1/2$ inch with each number. There are approximately 20 yards between the distance of consecutive clubs. The distances below are averages and players may hit longer or shorter.

Club	Loft (Degrees)	Approx. Shaft Length (Inches)	Approx. Distance (Yards)
Driver	10	43.5	250
1 Wood	12	43	230
2 Wood	16	42.5	210
3 Wood	20	42	190
4 Wood	24	41.5	170
5 Wood	28	41	160
2 Iron	18	38.5	200
3 Iron	22	38	190
4 Iron	26	37.5	180
5 Iron	30	37	170
6 Iron	34	36.5	160
7 Iron	38	36	150
8 Iron	42	35.5	140
9 Iron	46	35	130
Pitching Wedge	52	35	100
Sand Wedge	58	35	80

125. GOLF CLUB DIAGRAMS

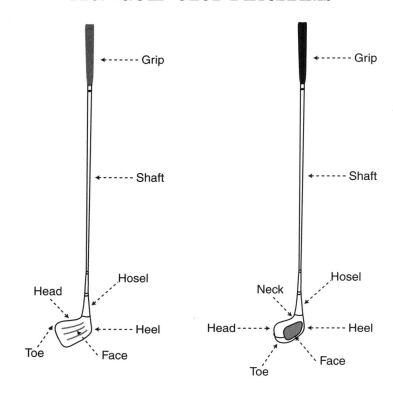

126. GOLF BALLS AND TEES

→ Flight characteristics of golf balls, such as spin and trajectory, vary according to their construction.

→ Basically, golf balls are either hard or soft.

→ Hard golf balls have a low trajectory, little spin, and tend to roll on impact which can result in greater distance.

→ The lack of spin also reduces hooks and slices.

→ Soft golf balls have a higher trajectory and spin that tend to minimize roll, and promote control and accuracy.

→ The compression rating for a golf ball is usually expressed as 90 or 100.

→ Since there is no standard rating scale, the compression rating simply indicates an individual manufacturer's soft or hard golf ball.

Ball Types

→ *Wound Balata*—A 3-piece ball with a gel core wrapped in elastic bindings and encased in a balata shell. Low handicap competition golfers prefer them because of their soft feel and spin characteristics. The shell is delicate which leads to rapid tearing and a general loss of shape on impact.

→ *3-Piece Balls*—Made from a solid rubber core wrapped in elastic bindings and encased in suryln, these balls are soft and offer a high degree of feel; however, they are not particularly durable. A good ball for players looking for control rather than distance.

→ *2-Piece Balls*—Made from a solid rubber core encased in suryln, these balls are slightly hard. These are the most common ball because they offer a good compromise among durability, distance, feel, and control.

→ *1-Piece Ball*—A solid surlyn ball that is very hard and only used for practice.

→ *Double Covered Ball*—A 2- or 3-piece ball covered in an extra shell. These are said to be soft yet durable, have spin that is good for control, and loft that is not good for distance.

Tees

→ Tees are made of wood and come in various lengths.

→ The standard length is $2^{1}/_{8}$ inches.

127. BASIC GOLF GRIP

➡ The golf grip is the only means of contact with the club and, ultimately, the ball. A proper grip is essential to a controlled and constant swing.

➡ The goal is to adopt a relaxed but firm grip that prevents any twisting of the shaft, causing the club face to open or close at the moment of impact with the ball.

➡ The overlapping golf grip is the most commonly used golf grip. Left-handed golfers use the same grip using their opposite hands.

➡ Lay the club diagonally across the palm of the left hand, starting with the middle knuckle of the forefinger and ending with the base of the little finger.

➡ Close the left hand around the grip with the thumb slightly right of the center of the shaft. The club face should be parallel to the back of the hand.

➡ Bring the right hand to the shaft so that the grip rests on the middle joints of the second and third fingers. The little finger can either interlock or overlap the forefinger of the left hand.

➡ Close the right hand around the grip with the thumb resting left of the shaft's center. The palm of the right hand should now be parallel to the backside of the left hand.

➡ The little finger of the right hand should overlap the forefinger of the left hand.

128. BASIC GOLF SWING

There are five stages to the golf swing—address, take away, backswing, downswing, and follow through. The eyes should be focused on the ball at all times.

Address

➡ To address the ball is to assume the correct stance and posture. Stand over the ball with the feet parallel to the intended ball trajectory and bring the club head to the ball.

Take Away

➡ The take away is the first part of the backswing.

➡ The club is brought parallel to the ground simply by moving the shoulders.

➡ Hands and arms remain in the same basic positions as at address.

➡ Weight is transferred to the back leg as the front foot lifts at the heel.

Backswing

➡ The club head is brought over the head as the hands extend to shoulder height.

➡ The wrists should be cocked at the top of the backswing.

➡ Weight is almost entirely transferred to the back leg.

➡ The front leg will only be touching the ground with the ball of the foot.

Downswing

➡ The downswing is that part of the swing from the top of the backswing to the point of impact with the ball.

➡ The unwinding of the hips drives the action.

➡ The upper body and legs follow the hips and weight is transferred from back to front.

➡ The arms are extended and the wrists are uncocked.

➡ As the club impacts the ball, weight should be slightly balanced on the front side.

Follow Through

➡ The follow through is that part of the swing during and after impact with the ball.

➡ The body uncoils fully with the back hip and shoulder pointing at the ball's original position and the body facing down the target line.

➡ The arms follow through to bring the club head around the back of the head.

➡ The club head should pull the ball along the target line.

➡ If the club head moves from out to in or vice versa, the ball will be either pulled or pushed along its line of flight.

129. HOW TO PUTT

While techniques of putting vary widely, the concentration and confidence required and the basic fundamentals used are the same in every player's putting stroke.

Address

➡ Stand over the ball with your feet parallel to the intended ball trajectory.

➡ The ball should be between the front foot and the center of your stance.

➡ The eyes should be directly over the ball.

➡ The elbows should be in against the hips and the knees should be flexed.

➡ The rest of the body should be relaxed but upright.

Take Away

➡ The club head is brought back as far as the back foot with a smooth action.

➡ The action is performed solely by the upper body with the arms and wrists following.

➡ The lower body and head are kept absolutely still.

Impact

➡ The club is brought to the ball with a smooth stroke (which returns it to the address position).

➡ The upper body does the work, with the arms, hands, and club following.

➡ The lower body and head should be kept absolutely still.

Follow Through

➡ After contact, the ball is pushed forward by the putter.

➡ The arms, hands, and putter follow.

➡ The lower body and head are kept still.

➡ Looking up at the ball directly after impact causes the swing plane to alter and the ball to be pushed off the target line.

130. GOLF TERMS

Ace	A hole in one.
Address	A golfer takes his or her stance and lines up the club to make a stroke.
Attend the Flag	To hold and remove the flagstick from the hole as an opponent putts.
Birdie	One under par for the hole.
Bogey	One over par for the hole.
Bunker	A hazard filled with sand or grass. Practice swings and grounding the club are not permitted in a bunker.
Chip	Hitting the ball into the air with enough flight to land on the green and roll across the green towards the hole.
Closed Face	Turning the club face slightly inward in order to hook the ball or prevent a slice.
Club Loft	The angle of the club face that affects the flight and distance of the ball when struck.
Divot	A piece of turf typically on the fairway and lifted when the ball is struck.
Dogleg	A hole where the fairway hooks to the left or right.
Double Bogey	Two shots over par for the hole.
Double Eagle	Three shots under par for the hole.
Draw	To induce topspin onto the ball causing it to move from outside to inside on the swing.
Eagle	To score two under par for a hole.
Face	The part of the club head that comes into direct contact with the ball.
Fade	To induce backspin onto the ball, causing it to travel through the air following inside to outside swing.
Fairway	The playing area between the tee and the green, which does not include hazards.
Fore	A warning to other players that a ball may hit them.
Green	The area of short grass surrounding the hole.
Grounding the Club	To place the club on the ground prior to striking the ball when addressing it.
Handicap	The number of strokes a player is given to adjust his or her score to that of standard scratch. It allows golfers of different abilities to compete on equal terms.
Head	The end of the club that includes the club face.
Heel	Where the club head is attached to the shaft.
Hole in One	The ball goes straight into the hole from the tee shot.

Hook	To induce topspin onto the ball causing it to move from outside to inside on the swing.
Lateral Water Hazard	A water hazard that runs parallel to the fairway.
Lip	The edge of the hole.
Loft	The angle of the club face in relation to the ground which dictates the trajectory of the ball as it rises in the air.
Mulligan	When a player is allowed to replay any one shot per hole.
OB	Acronym for Out of Bounds.
Out of Bounds	The area on or adjacent to the course from which the ball may not be played. Usually marked by white posts.
Par	The number of shots a low handicapper should take for a hole or round. Par for a hole is measured by the number of shots needed to reach the green plus two for the putting. Par for a round is calculated by adding all of the hole's pars together.
Penalty Stroke	A stroke added to a player's score due to a rule infringement.
Pin	The pole with a flag attached in the hole on the green.
Pitch	The ball is hit high into the air onto the green using a lofted club.
Provisional Ball	Playing a second ball from the same place as the first because the player is unsure of where the first ball may have landed.
Putt	Act of hitting a golf ball towards the hole on the green.
Rough	High grass area adjacent to the fairway and green.
Shaft	The part of the club between the head and the grip.
Slice	To induce too much backspin onto the ball, causing it to travel through the air following an inside to outside swing.
Sole	The underside of the club head.
Sole Plate	The metal underside of a wood's club head.
Spike Mark	A tuft of grass caused by spiked shoes.
Stance	To place the feet in preparation for a swing.
Tee	A small peg stuck into the ground on which a golf ball is placed. Also, the area where golfers play the first stroke of any given hole.
Tending the Flag	To hold the flagstick in such a way that a player may aim for it. It must be removed as a putt approaches.
Toe	That part of the club head at the opposite end to the heel.

131. HISTORICAL FACTS ABOUT GYMNASTICS AND TUMBLING

→ The word "gymnastics" comes from the Greek word *gymnazein*, which means "exercising without clothes."

→ Gymnastics as we know it began in Sweden during the beginning of the 1800s.

→ Germany and Czechoslovakia developed the event apparatus around the same time.

→ Friedrich Ludwig Jahn invented parallel and horizontal bars, the rings, the horse, and the balance beam in Germany in early 1800.

→ Gymnastics became very popular, and the sport quickly spread throughout Europe.

→ Immigrants to the United States were responsible for the growth of gymnastics in the U.S. after the Civil War.

→ Gymnastics for men were included in the 1896 Olympic Games.

→ Competition for women began 40 years later.

132. BASIC FACTS ABOUT GYMNASTICS COMPETITION

Three Segments of Competition

→ **Team**—Each of six members performs a compulsory and an optional routine on each apparatus. The five highest scores on each apparatus are added together for a team total. The team with the highest number of points wins.

→ **All-around**—The best gymnasts from each team perform an optional routine on each piece of apparatus. Individual scores are totaled and the gymnast with the most points is declared the winner.

→ **Individual**—The gymnasts with the highest number of points on each piece of apparatus compete again on optionals. The gymnast with the most number of points on each piece of equipment is the winner.

Three Areas Considered by Judges When Scoring Gymnastics

→ Difficulty: The difficulty rating of the stunt being performed.

→ Composition: The way in which the routine is put together.

→ Execution: How the routine is performed.

133. EVENTS INCLUDED IN GYMNASTICS COMPETITION

Men

→ Floor Exercise

→ Horizontal Bar

→ Parallel Bars

→ Pommel Horse

→ Rings

→ Vault

Women

→ Floor Exercise

→ Balance Beam

→ Uneven Parallel Bars

→ Vault

Floor Exercise

→ Women must use music with no words, and men may not use music.

→ The size of the floor is about 10 by 10 meters (40 by 40 feet).

→ There is a white line along the perimeter of the mat, and deductions are given if the gymnast steps out of that line.

→ Gymnasts must have a routine that consists of dance moves and tumbling runs.

→ A routine for women must be 70 to 90 seconds; for men, it must be 50 to 70 seconds.

Balance Beam

→ There is no music, and a beam routine must be 70 to 90 seconds long.

→ The balance beam is about 16 1/2 feet long, about 4 inches wide, and about 4 feet from the floor.

→ Beams are made out of wood or aluminum.

→ A gymnast's routine must consist of difficult skills and dance movements.

→ A gymnast is scored on execution of the skills, elegance of the performance, and flow of the routine.

Uneven Parallel Bars

→ There is no music in this event.

→ The bars consist of two round wooden poles held by metal uprights.

→ The low bar is 5 feet from the ground, and the high bar is 7 1/2 feet from the ground.

→ The distance between the two bars varies from gymnast to gymnast, depending on her height and the skill being performed.

→ A routine on the bars must consist of a certain number of skills, depending on the level.

→ During a routine, a gymnast changes direction, uses both bars, and performs various skills, including flight elements where the gymnast completely releases and regrasps the bars.

→ The routine must be free flowing with no stops and each move must be done cleanly to receive full marks.

Vault

→ There is no music and both men and women use the same vaults, except that the women vault sideways, and the men vault long ways.

→ For women, the vault is $4^1/_2$ feet; for men, the vault is $5^1/_2$ feet high.

→ Women are permitted 78 feet to run; men are permitted 65 feet.

→ Gymnasts run and jump off a beatboard or springboard to perform.

→ The springboard can be various distances away from the vault, depending on the gymnast and the difficulty of the skill.

→ Women are permitted two attempts; men are permitted one.

→ In the finals for both men and women, the gymnasts are permitted two vaults, and their scores are averaged to form a final mark.

Pommel Horse

→ Similar to the vault, except that the horse has two wooden handles, called pommels, on top.

→ The pommel horse is 3 feet 8 inches off the floor, and approximately 5 feet long.

→ The pommels are 5 inches upright.

→ A routine consists of many difficult strength skills linked together, and performed cleanly on the pommels.

Horizontal Bar

→ It is similar to the other two bar events (uneven parallel bars for women, and parallel bars for men), but consists of only one bar.

→ The horizontal bar is made of metal. It is 8 feet long and $8^1/_2$ feet from the ground.

→ A routine consists of many swing and release moves.

→ A gymnast should have a change in direction and a change of grip.

Rings

→ It consists of a set of two rings, which are $8^1/_2$ feet from the ground.

→ The cables that hold the rings are connected to the ceiling, or are at least 18 feet from the floor.

→ The rings are made out of wood with laminated cover, or fiberglass, and are suspended from long nylon or leather straps.

→ A routine is composed of swing elements, hanging elements, and handstands.

Parallel Bars

→ The bars have a rectangular shape, with rounded edges.

→ The parallel bars are made of wood or fiberglass poles, and are parallel to each other.

→ They are 5 feet 9 inches from the ground, and 11 feet long.

→ A routine on the parallel bars should consist of a mount, handstands, swings, somersaults, and a dismount.

134. BASIC GYMNASTICS SKILLS

➤ Positions used while performing different stunts include:
- Tuck—The chin is down and the knees and hips are bent.
- Pike—The torso is bent at the hips and the legs are straight.
- Layout—The entire body is straight.
- Puck—A combination of the tuck and the pike with only a slight bend in the knees.

➤ Grasps used while performing on the apparatus include:
- Over grasp—The palms of the hand are on top of the bar.
- Under grasp—The palms of the hand are under the bar.
- Mixed grasp—One hand is over the bar and the other hand is under the bar.

➤ Basic movements in gymnastics include:
- Somersault—A rotation around the body's horizontal axis.
- Twist—A rotation around the body's vertical axis.
- Kip—A quick flex and then extension of the body.
- Extension—An extension and then flexion of the body.

135. SAFETY RULES FOR GYMNASTICS AND TUMBLING CLASSES

➤ An instructor must be present before tumbling or performing skills are performed on the equipment.

➤ Warm-ups must be performed before each class and participants must allow enough time to cool down after class.

➤ Make certain not to perform when ill or injured.

➤ Proper clothing must be worn for safe participation.

➤ Only attempt skills that are within your ability level.

➤ Make certain to always follow proper progression of skills.

➤ Be attentive to the person you are spotting and the skill being performed.

➤ Make certain any problems have been discussed and understood by the instructor and performer before a new skill is attempted.

➤ Always use proper safety mats and safety procedures when performing.

➤ Do not distract others while they are performing or are getting ready to perform.

➤ Use spotters when performing any skill.

➤ Be aware of your limitations in respect to excessive weight on the neck, lateral flexion of the knees or elbows, and undue strain on the shoulders, spine, ankles, and wrists.

➤ Make certain there is adequate space when performing running skills and somersaults.

136. GYMNASTICS AND TUMBLING TERMS

Ariel A cartwheel with no hands. A gymnast hurdles off one foot and lands on one foot.

Back Handspring Usually done out of a round-off on floor, the gymnast jumps backward, lands on his or her hands in a handstand, and then pops down back onto his or her feet.

Barani A front flip with a half twist.

Cast From a front support on the bar, the gymnast kicks his or her legs out from under, and then comes back to the bar.

Giants Swings around the bar with the body perfectly straight. It is often the skill before a release move or dismount.

Hurdle A run or a step to position the feet for takeoff, usually done in the beginning of a move.

Mount The first skill(s) of a routine.

Pike The gymnast's legs are straight, and the body is bent forward as much as possible.

Round-off A cartwheel, with a push off the hands and two-foot landing.

"Stuck" Landing When a gymnast completes a move and finishes the move without talking any extra steps.

Tinsica A cross between a cartwheel and a front walkover.

Tuck The knees are really close to the chest, and the arms are around them, holding them there.

Tumbling Line A line in which three or more skills are performed in succession, starting with a run for power.

137. HISTORICAL FACTS ABOUT HANDBALL

➡ Handball is referred to in Homer's *The Odyssey*. Homer described players in a game the ancient Greeks called *urania.*

➡ The Romans played a ball game called *harpaston* in which players threw the ball to teammates while trying to avoid opposing players.

➡ In the Middle Ages, German lyrical poet Walther von der Vogelweide referred to a similar game called *catch ball.*

➡ In France in the 1500s, François Rabelais described a type of handball where they played ball using the palm of their hand.

➡ Rules and methods of play were written in Denmark by 1848.

➡ German gymnastics instructor Konrad Koch developed a handball sport called *Raffball,* or *snatch ball,* in 1897.

➡ Sweden first used the name *handball* in 1910.

➡ The German general secretary of the International Football Association began encouraging handball in 1912 as a method of keeping football players fit during the off-season.

➡ Germany and Austria played the first international handball match in 1925, with Germany winning 6–3.

➡ The International Amateur Handball Federation was formed in 1928, and, by 1936, it had 23 member countries.

➡ The sport arrived at the 1928 Olympic Games in Berlin.

➡ The sport was dropped from the Olympic Games after World War II, but the game was reinstituted for men in 1972 and for women in 1976.

➡ Handball is currently played in 145 officially recognized countries, with over 8 million players registered worldwide.

138. HANDBALL EQUIPMENT

Ball

➠ The ball is made of rubber or synthetic material and is uniform in color.

➠ It is round, $1^7/_8$ inches in diameter, and weighs 2.3 ounces.

➠ A lighter ball may be used in various levels of play.

Gloves

➠ Gloves must be worn.

➠ Gloves must be light in color and made of a soft material or leather.

➠ The fingers may not be webbed, connected, or removed.

➠ No foreign substance, such as tape or rubber bands, may be used on the fingers or on the palms on the outside of the gloves.

➠ Metal or hard substances may not be worn under the glove.

➠ Gloves with holes that expose the skin may not be worn.

Eye Protection

➠ Protective eyewear must be properly worn at all times during play.

➠ Failure to wear appropriate protective eyewear properly will result in a technical and the player will be charged a timeout to secure eyewear.

➠ The second violation in the same match will result in a forfeit.

139. HANDBALL COURT AND BASIC RULES

The standard three-wall and four-wall courts for handball are 40 feet long, 20 feet wide, and 20 feet high. One-wall handball courts typically measure 20 feet wide, 16 feet high, and 34 feet long. Players may use only one hand at a time to play the ball. The server drops the ball on the floor in the service zone and hits the ball so that it hits the front wall and rebounds into the back court. The opponent returns the ball on the fly or first bounce so that it hits the front wall, either directly or off a side wall, and rebounds to return the ball legally. The first side scoring 21 points wins the game.

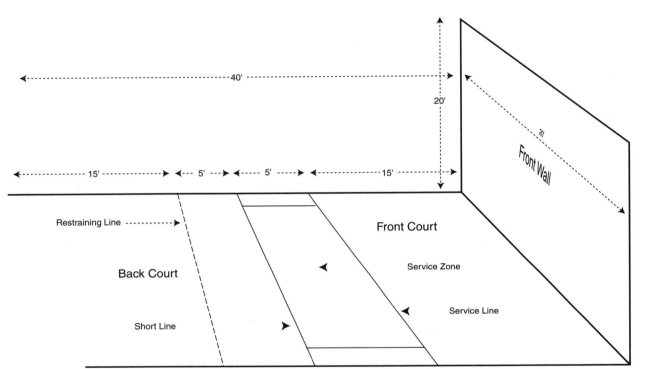

140. BASIC RULES OF TEAM HANDBALL

General Rules

➡ Handball is a fast-paced game involving two teams of seven players who pass, throw, catch, and dribble a small ball with their hands while trying to score goals.

➡ The team with more goals wins the game.

➡ A game consists of two 30-minute halves with a 10-minute half-time break.

➡ The game starts with a throw-off, where a player stands with one foot on the center line and throws the ball to a teammate behind the line, signaling that each team may move into its opponent's side of the court.

➡ The player receiving the ball must be at least three meters away.

➡ The throw-off is the method of starting play after every goal, as well as the start of the second half.

➡ The offense tries to throw the ball past the opposing goalkeeper and into a goal three meters wide and two meters high.

➡ Only the goalkeeper may enter the goal area.

➡ Players may use any part of their bodies except their lower legs and feet to stop, hit, catch, or throw the ball.

➡ They may not touch the ball twice in a row unless dribbling it, fumbling it, or passing it from one hand to the other, meaning, in effect, they may not throw it to themselves.

➡ Players can hold the ball for only three seconds before passing, dribbling, or shooting.

➡ Players may take only three steps after catching the ball. If players dribble, they may only take another three steps.

➡ Three meters is the distance for free throws and penalty throws.

Fouls and Penalties

➡ A free throw is awarded for playing the ball illegally.

➡ Free throws are the right to play the ball without interference, although the person with the free throw may try to shoot instead of pass.

➡ A player takes the free throw on the spot where the offense occurred, unless it occurred inside the free-throw line.

➡ If it occurred inside the free-throw line, the player moves back to the free-throw line, allowing defenders to stand back the required three meters and still stand outside the goal area, which is reserved for the goalkeeper.

➡ A penalty throw is awarded for illegal interference by a defender that prevents a shot at goal, or a defender playing the ball back into the goal area and the goalkeeper touching it.

➡ The offensive player takes the penalty throw from the penalty line seven meters in front of the goal.

➡ The goalkeeper, the only person allowed to defend against the throw, may advance as far as the goalkeeper's restraining line, while maintaining the 3-meter distance.

➡ The players are allowed to obstruct other players with their bodies whether or not they have the ball.

➡ Players may not steal or strike the ball from other players, obstruct them with their arms or legs, or treat them roughly.

Throw-ins, Goal Throws, and Corner Throws

➡ If the ball goes out of bounds over the sidelines, the team that did not touch it last is allowed a throw-in from that spot.

➡ If a ball that was last touched by an offensive player or the defending goalkeeper goes over the back line, the goalkeeper is awarded a goal throw-out to a teammate.

➡ If a defender touched it last, the attacking team gets a corner throw.

➡ If play stops for a reason where neither side is to blame, or the ball hits the ceiling, a referee throws to restart play.

➡ The referee throws the ball into the air, and a player from each team jumps for it.

Additional Rules

➡ Goalkeepers within the goal area are not limited in how many times they may touch the ball or how many steps they can take with the ball.

➡ Goalkeepers may defend the goal with any part of their bodies, including their feet.

➡ All lines on the court are considered in play.

➡ Players may not put the ball out of play deliberately.

➡ Players may be warned for fouls or misconduct (yellow card), suspended for two minutes, or, for serious or continual offenses, disqualified from a match (red card).

➡ After two minutes, a substitute may replace the disqualified player.

➡ Teams have five substitutes.

➡ Players may be substituted at any time, as often as desired.

➡ Each team is allowed a 1-minute timeout per half.

141. HISTORICAL FACTS ABOUT HOPSCOTCH

➡ The original hopscotch courts were over 100 feet long and were used for military training exercises during the early Roman Empire.

➡ Roman foot soldiers ran the course in full armor and field packs in order to improve their footwork.

➡ Roman children imitated the soldiers by drawing their own patterns and creating their own scoring system.

➡ There are still hopscotch patterns scratched in the pavement of the old Forum in Rome.

➡ Pliny the Elder (who died in the year 79 A.D.) tells of the boys in his time playing hopscotch.

➡ Later, Christians thought the game represented the progress of the soul from Earth to Heaven and called the last square *paradise.*

➡ Even today, the last square is sometimes rounded to represent the dome of Heaven.

➡ Romans brought the game to England where it spread throughout Europe and ultimately to America.

➡ The game is called *Marelles* in France, *Templehupfen* in Germany, *Hinklebaan* in the Netherlands, *Ekaria Dukaria* in India, *Pico* in Vietnam, and *Rayuela* in Argentina.

142. HOW TO PLAY HOPSCOTCH

➡ Hopscotch patterns are usually found in playgrounds, but can be created on almost any flat surface with chalk or string.

➡ In order to begin the game, each player must start with a marker.

➡ The first player tosses his or her marker into the first square.

➡ The marker must land completely within the designated square without touching a line or bouncing out.

➡ If the marker lands in the wrong square, the player forfeits his or her turn.

➡ If the marker is successful, the player hops through the court, beginning on square one.

➡ If the squares are side by side, they must be straddled, with the left foot landing in the left square and the right foot landing in the right square.

➡ Single squares must be hopped in on one foot.

➡ For the first single square, either foot may be used, but that same foot must be used throughout the court and back.

➡ A player must always hop over any square where a marker has been placed.

➡ Squares marked *safe, home,* or *rest* are neutral squares, and may be hopped through in any manner without penalty.

➡ When a player reaches the end of the court, he or she must turn around and hop back through the court, moving through the squares in reverse order and bending to pick up his or her marker on the way back.

➡ Sometimes a dome-shaped "rest area" is added on one end of the hopscotch pattern where the player can rest for a second or two before hopping back through.

➡ Upon successfully completing the sequence, the player continues his or her turn by tossing his or her marker into square number two, and repeating the pattern.

➡ If, while hopping through the court in either direction, the player steps on a line, misses a square, or loses balance, his or her turn ends.

➡ The player puts the marker in the square where he or she will resume playing on the next turn, and the next player begins.

➡ The first player to complete one course for every numbered square on the pattern wins the game.

➡ There are hundreds of pattern variations that can be drawn.

➡ Chalk can be used on the ground or masking tape can be used on a floor to draw a hopscotch pattern.

➡ The hopscotch pattern should be created with at least 8 numbered sections.

➡ Each player should have a marker such as a stone, beanbag, bottlecap, shell, button, etc.

➡ Squares can be any size and should be adjusted for age and ability, but approximately 18 to 24 inches per square is the recommended size.

143. BASIC HOPSCOTCH PATTERNS

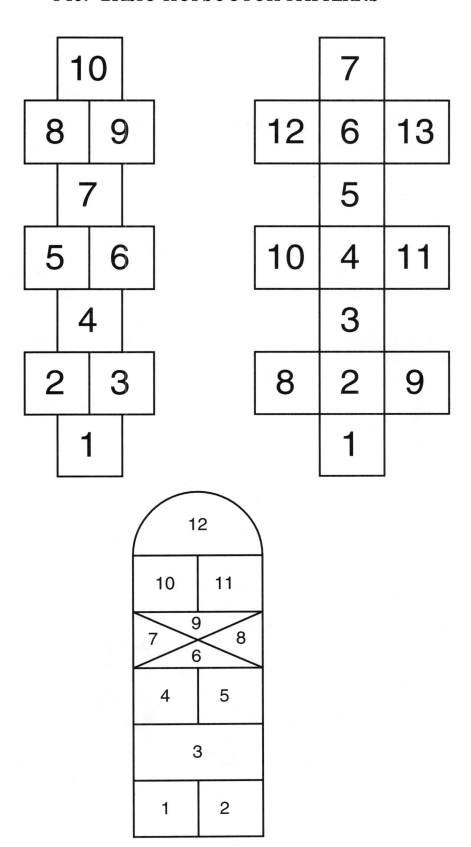

144. HISTORICAL FACTS ABOUT HORSESHOES

➡ As early as the second century, before the Christian era, iron plates or rings for shoes were nailed on horses' feet in Western Asia and Eastern Europe.

➡ Camp followers of the Grecian armies, who could not afford the discus, took discarded horseshoes, set up a stake, and began throwing horseshoes at it.

➡ Following the American Revolutionary War, England's Duke of Wellington said, "The War was won by pitchers of horse hardware."

➡ England set up rules in 1869 to govern the game.

➡ The game was a favorite among soldiers in most wars.

➡ The first horseshoe-pitching tournament in which competition was open to the world was held in the summer of 1910 in Bronson, Kansas.

➡ The first ruling body of horseshoe pitching of which any record was found was organized in a courtroom of the First District Court, Kansas City, Kansas on May 16, 1914.

➡ The National League of Horseshoe and Quoit Pitchers was organized at the National Tournament in St. Petersburg, Florida on February 26, 1919, with representatives from 29 different states attending.

➡ It is estimated that upwards of fifteen million enthusiasts enjoy pitching horseshoes in the United States and Canada.

145. HORSESHOE EQUIPMENT AND COURTS

The Horseshoe

→ The horseshoe may not weigh more than 2 pounds 10 ounces.

→ The horseshoe may not exceed $7\frac{1}{4}$ inches in width.

→ The horseshoe may not exceed $7\frac{5}{8}$ inches in length.

→ On a parallel line $\frac{3}{4}$ inch from a straight edge touching the points of the shoe, the opening of the shoe may not exceed $3\frac{1}{2}$ inches.

The Courts

→ Stakes are placed 40 feet apart.

→ Stakes should extend 14 to 15 inches above the pit surface.

→ Stakes may be inclined toward each other, but not more than a 3-inch lean.

→ Stakes should be solid or hollow steel 1 inch in diameter.

→ Stakes should be a minimum of 21 inches from the front and back of the pit.

→ Pits should be 31 to 36 inches wide and 43 to 72 inches deep.

→ If the pit is less than the maximum dimensions, the extra space should be filled with the same material of which the platforms are made and should be level with the pit and platforms.

→ The stake should be at the center of the pit.

→ Pits are best filled with clay, which must be watered periodically to maintain its texture.

→ Sand, sawdust, and loose soil are more commonly used.

→ Any material that keeps the shoes from bouncing excessively can be used.

→ Minimum depth of the substance is 4 inches, but 8 inches are recommended.

→ A foul line is marked three feet in front of each stake.

→ The throwing distance (foul line to opposite stake) is 37 feet.

→ The foul line is 27 feet from the opposite stake for female, junior, and elderly contestants.

Backboards

→ The backboard should be at least four feet behind the stake.

→ The backboard should be at least 1 foot high and extend the width of the pit.

146. HORSESHOE COURT DIAGRAMS

The standard court is 6 by 46 feet, with a pit at each end. The stakes are 40 feet apart with a foul line three feet in front of each stake. Women, juniors (17 and under), and seniors pitch from 30 feet with the foul line 27 feet from the target stake.

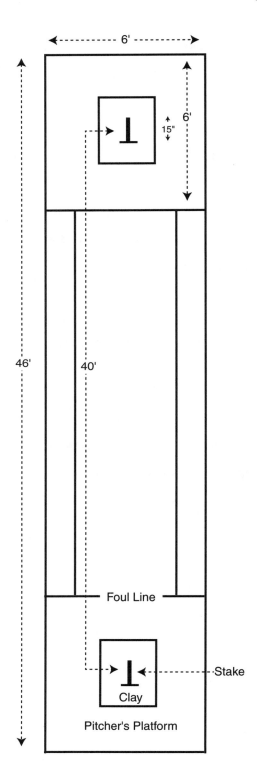

© 2001 Parker Publishing Company

147. HORSESHOE PITCHING TECHNIQUES

➡ The player stands to one side opposite the stake.

➡ The player stands erect and well balanced.

➡ The shoe is gripped with the index or forefinger and middle fingers underneath and the first joints of the fingers curved up over the edge of the inner circle of the shoe.

➡ The shoe extends to full-arm length in front.

➡ The player holds the shoe, with the caulks down, at about a 45-degree angle to the ground.

➡ The player swings the shoe up on a level with the eyes and sights it at the opposite stake.

➡ The player bends slightly at the knees, leans forward at the waist, and swings the shoe easily backward.

➡ The player steps forward with the foot that is opposite the delivery arm a split second before the backswing is completed.

➡ The shoe does not pause at the end of the backswing.

➡ The arm swings forward, straight from the shoulder, in a pendulum movement.

➡ As the shoe passes the standing leg in the frontswing, the player brings it to a level position with a free, natural roll of the arm.

➡ At this exact moment, the body weight is shifted smoothly to the opposite foot.

➡ The nonweight-bearing knee straightens up to its natural position and the body rises with the swing.

➡ The player releases the shoe as it swings up in line with the eyes and the opposite stake.

➡ Released in a level position, the shoe leaves the hand cleanly with no jerk or snap of the arm and wrist.

➡ The release point should correspond with the aim point.

➡ After releasing the shoe, the player's hand swings up, above the head, in a graceful follow-through.

➡ All movements should be smooth and well coordinated.

➡ The shoe floats lazily through the air in an arc that is about 8 feet high at its highest point. (The height of the trajectory varies with different players.)

➡ The shoe lands flat with little or no rebound.

➡ If the shoe is pitched too low and too swiftly, it cannot open properly.

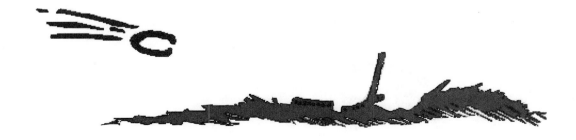

148. BASIC RULES OF HORSESHOES

General Rules

➡ Each player pitches both shoes, then his or her opponent pitches both shoes.

➡ In pitching a shoe, the player may not cross the foul line.

➡ When playing teams, half the team throws from one stake and half throws from the other.

➡ Games can be played to 40 points in a point-limit game or 40 shoes in a shoe-limit game.

➡ In the shoe-limit game, the player with the highest points wins.

➡ If a tie exists, then each player can take a half win or a two-inning tie-breaker can be thrown.

Scoring

➡ Any shoe must be within one horseshoe-width (measured across the outside of the open end of the shoe) of the stake to be considered for points.

➡ Official rules call for a maximum of six inches between shoe and stake to be considered for points.

➡ The closest shoe to the stake gets 1 point.

➡ If two of one player's shoes are closer than any of the opponent's, that player gets 2 points.

➡ Ringers are worth 3 points each and must completely encircle the stake so the ends can be touched with a straight-edge without touching the stake.

➡ If a player has the closest shoe and a ringer, it's 4 points.

➡ If a player's opponent throws a ringer on top of his or her opponent's ringer, they cancel each other and no points are scored.

➡ Leaners are worth 1 point and are considered closer than any adjacent shoe except ringers.

149. INTERESTING FACTS ABOUT JACKS

➡ The game of jacks is also known as *jackstones, chuckstones, dibs, dab, fivestones*, and *knucklebones*.

➡ The name knucklebone is derived from when the game was originally played with the small bones from the knees of sheep.

➡ Jacks was played in ancient Greece and Rome, and it is believed to have been played for centuries before that.

➡ The appeal of the game of jacks appears to be the contrast between its simplicity combined with the level of skill necessary for success.

150. FLIPPING THE JACKS

➡ A player takes all the jacks in the palms of the two hands held together.

➡ The player throws the jacks into the air as he or she turns the hands over so that the backs of the hands are upwards with the index fingers touching.

➡ This forms a surface onto which the player will catch the jacks.

➡ The jacks are thrown into the air again, this time returning the hands to the palms-up position at which he or she started.

➡ When flipping for first, the player who drops the least goes first.

➡ If none drop, players take turns flipping until someone drops a jack, determining who goes first.

151. BASIC RULES OF JACKS

→ Players *flip* the jacks to determine who goes first.

→ Players begin by throwing the jacks out on the floor.

→ Using the little ball that comes in the sets or a tennis-ball sized pink rubber ball (pinkie ball), the player throws the ball into the air, picks up the correct number of jacks, lets the ball bounce once, and catches the ball while still holding the jack(s) that were just picked up.

→ Players may use only one hand.

→ A player's turn continues until he or she misses the ball, misses the jacks, moves a jack, or drops a jack that was picked up on that play.

→ When the player is out, the next person begins his or her turn.

→ For *onesies*, a player picks up one jack at a time, until he or she collects all ten.

→ Players may put the jacks they have collected into their other hand or on the ground before he or she attempts to collect more.

→ For *twosies*, a player picks up two jacks at a time, until he or she has collected all ten.

→ For *threesies,* a player picks up the jacks three at a time, and then the one jack that is left over, until he or she has collected all ten. Any leftover jacks are picked up after all the others have been collected in that group of ten.

→ If players pick up any leftovers before their opponent has picked up all the evenly grouped jacks, they are putting the horse before the cart and therefore must call "cart" as they take the leftover jack(s).

→ On *foursies*, there are two groups of four and two jacks in the "cart."

→ *Fivesies* has no cart.

→ *Sixsies* has one group of six and four in the "cart," etc.

→ If players throw the jacks and two (or more) are touching, it is called *kissies* and players have the option of picking up the kissing jacks and dropping them to spread them out.

→ The first player to complete the challenge of going from *onsies* to *tensies* and back down again to *onsies* is the winner.

152. HISTORICAL FACTS ABOUT JUGGLING

"If you can scramble an egg, tie your own shoelaces, or stumble onto the light switch at night . . . then you can learn how to juggle!"

—*Juggling for the Complete Klutz,* John Cassidy and B.C. Rimbeaux,
Klutz Press, Palo Alto, CA, 1977

➡ The first graphic representations of jugglers appear on early Egyptian wall paintings and Greek vases.

➡ A statue in the National Museum in Athens, Greece, which was found in the Pyrénées, also attests to the antiquity of juggling.

➡ Hermann Sagemüller writes of an officer in a Roman Legion who entertained his troops by performing juggling tricks.

➡ One of the oldest props in juggling, the diabolo (the devil on two sticks) had its beginning in China.

➡ The diabolo is a spool resembling two cones fastened so that the narrower point is in the center which is manipulated by means of a string attached to two sticks.

➡ The spinning of plates on slender rods has been popular with the Chinese for centuries.

➡ The Japanese preferred to toss little sticks and balance, roll, and bounce a medium-sized ball on various parts of the body.

➡ Jugglers of the Orient often used props that were shaped to depict birds, fish, and other animals.

➡ Additional movement and flexibility were achieved by joining different parts of the animals with hinge-like devices, creating the illusion of flapping wings and wiggling tails.

➡ In England, at the time of William the Conqueror, the title "The King of the Jugglers" appeared and continued to appear for over four centuries. Many privileges went along with the title, which was conferred by statute.

➡ The word *juggler* in old England was very broad in meaning and could have applied to musician, poet, or any enterprising showman who had gained the favors of the court.

153. HOW TO JUGGLE

Step 1: The Toss

➡ Use three balls that are heavy for their size, approximately the size and weight of a small apple.

➡ The weight is important in order for the juggler to properly feel the balls land in the hand.

➡ Tennis balls are too light, golf balls are too small, and softballs are too big for the novice.

➡ The juggler begins by imagining two spots, about a foot in front of his or her forehead, one to the right of the head, one to the left, about 8 inches apart.

➡ These spots are the juggler's focus points and are very important.

➡ The arms are held at waist level with the hands naturally out in front (the rest position).

➡ Starting with a ball in the right hand and the left hand empty, the ball is tossed across to the left imaginary spot and caught in the left hand.

➡ The ball should then be tossed back from the left hand across to the imaginary spot on the right and caught in the right hand.

Step 2: Hints for Success

➡ When the ball is tossed, it should be "popped" from the palm.

➡ The juggler should not let it roll off the fingertips.

➡ The ball is much more difficult to control if the juggler lets his or her fingers touch it.

➡ The juggler should not jerk the hand as the ball is "popped." The motion of the ball should be kept smooth.

➡ The juggler should watch that the ball is not spinning as it passes in front of his or her eyes.

➡ If the ball is spinning, this is an indication that the juggler probably let the ball roll off his or her fingers.

➡ Putting marks on the ball helps the juggler to check for spinning.

➡ The ball should be tossed from slightly inside of the natural resting position of the hands.

➡ When the ball is caught, it should be caught slightly outside of the resting position of the hands.

➡ The hands should be kept at waist level.

➡ Hands should not be allowed to drift up too far to catch or toss the ball.

➡ Focus should be kept on hitting the imaginary spots.

➡ The juggler should concentrate on not throwing too high or too low or too far out or too close to the body.

➡ If the ball is thrown reasonably well, the catching hand will know where the ball is and will catch it easily.

➡ The juggler should worry about tossing well, *not* about catching the ball.

➡ The ball should be caught in the palm of the hand.

➡ The juggler should not reach up and grab the ball, but let it fall into the hand.

➡ If the ball is heavy enough, it will stay in the hand.

➡ If the ball is too light, it will tend to bounce out of the hand.

➡ When the ball is caught, the juggler should pause for a moment and hold his or her hand at the spot where it was caught.

➡ The juggler should be catching the ball just a couple inches outside of the rest position of the hands.

➡ The juggler should note where the ball was caught and move the hand back to the rest position.

➡ Tossing the ball correctly is the key to successful juggling.

➡ The juggler should be patient, practice, and not proceed until he or she is catching the ball in the correct position consistently.

Step 3: Two-Ball Exchange

➡ The juggler holds two balls in the right hand, one towards the back of the palm, and one at the base of the first two fingers.

➡ The third ball is held in the left hand.

➡ The juggler starts with a two-ball exchange.

➡ The ball is tossed from the base of the fingers of the right hand.

➡ The initial toss is difficult to "pop" from the palm, so it is important to get a good starting toss from the base of the fingers.

➡ The juggler avoids rolling the ball off the fingertips, and works to hit the imaginary spot without any spin.

➡ When the ball just passes the spot and starts on its way down, the ball is popped up from the left hand (from slightly inside the rest position) and the first ball is caught as it comes down (the hand is slightly outside its rest position).

➡ The second ball is then caught in the right hand.

➡ Eyes are focused on the imaginary spots.

➡ The juggler should practice that sequence until it can be done repeatedly.

➡ If the juggler is not tossing well, refer to Step 2: Hints for Success before continuing.

Step 4: Three-Ball Exchange

➡ The juggler is now ready for the three-ball exchange.

➡ As the second ball passes its spot and is on the way down, the ball is tossed from the right hand and caught in the left.

➡ The juggler notes where his or her hands are when the balls are caught, and moves them back to their neutral position.

➡ The juggler must toss from the inside and catch on the outside.

➡ To help keep the timing consistent, say "left" and "right" as the balls are thrown from each hand.

➡ The juggler should practice until he or she can consistently catch the balls.

Step 5: Four-, Five-, etc., Ball Exchange

➡ The juggler repeats Step 4, adding one more toss each time he or she gets comfortable with a set of exchanges.

➡ The juggler continually reminds himself or herself of the basics from the earlier steps.

➡ The juggler begins to practice tossing the balls higher, lower, standing on one foot, closing the eyes, or juggling various items.

154. JUGGLING EXERCISES

One-Ball Exercise

➠ Start with one ball.

➠ Throw the ball in an arc from hand to hand about eye level.

➠ The pattern will be an arc, *not* a circle.

Two-Ball Exercise

➠ Start with one ball in each hand.

➠ Toss ball 1 in the right hand in the arc to about eye level to your left hand.

➠ When this ball 1 reaches the highest point in its arc, throw ball 2 in an arc from the left hand to the right.

➠ Catch ball 1 in the left hand.

➠ Then catch 2 in your right hand.

➠ Do this same exercise, except start with the left hand instead of the right.

➠ Practice until it can be done smoothly.

➠ Common mistakes include throwing two balls in a circle, or throwing both balls at the same time.

Three-Ball Exercise

➠ Start with two balls in one hand (1 and 3) (in this case the right hand, but if you are a lefty, use your left hand) and ball 2 in the other.

➠ Throw the ball in the front of your right hand in an arc to the left hand.

➠ When ball 1 reaches its highest point, throw ball 2 in the left hand in an arc to the right hand.

➠ Catch 1 in the left hand.

➠ When the ball thrown to the right hand reaches its height, throw ball 3 from the right hand in an arc to the left hand.

➠ Catch 2 in the right hand.

➠ It is helpful to roll ball 3 in the right hand to the front of the hand with a slight downward motion of the hand before it is thrown.

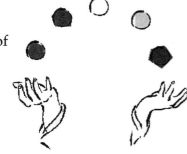

➠ When ball 3 reaches its highest point, throw ball 1 in the left hand in an arc to the right hand.

➠ Catch 3 in your left hand, etc.

155. HISTORICAL FACTS ABOUT JUMPING ROPE

➡ Many historians believe that when ancient Egyptian and Chinese rope makers were twisting long strands of hemp into ropes, they needed to jump over them to retrieve strands.

➡ The rope makers developed this skill and their children began to imitate and invent games with small pieces of rope.

➡ Traveling sailors, seeing the fun the children were having, took the ideas and games back to their own countries and children.

➡ Rope skipping was brought to America by Dutch settlers during the 1600s and has been written about by English settlers who migrated to New Amsterdam, later known as New York.

➡ Boys mainly performed rope skipping during the 1700s, as the culture of the time did not encourage girls to be physically active.

➡ With changes in the 1800s, both boys and girls were encouraged to play in games using skipping.

➡ Three types of skipping evolved during this time:

- single rope activities
- long rope with two turners
- double-dutch with two ropes turning in opposite directions

➡ As girls became more involved in rope skipping during the 1900s, they invented different rhythms and singing games, and it became a popular activity.

156. JUMP ROPE RHYMES

Jump roping is a unique part of our American cultural heritage. The American folk rhymes are mini-dramas, complete with violence; however, the violence is generally exaggerated beyond belief or can be useful in resolving problems that face jumpers, e.g., illnesses, boyfriends, sibling rivalries, etc. Other rhymes can be divided into three overlapping groups: those about domestic life, boyfriends, or about the game itself. The rhymes can be used to gently tease one another (Down in the valley where the green grass grows, there sat Mary, sweet as a rose), to brag (I love coffee, I love tea, I love the boys and the boys love me!), or to challenge an opponent to a new level of athleticism (How many pieces did she eat? 10, 20, 30). Reciting rhymes can help rope jumpers to keep their rhythm while jumping

A, B, C and vegetable goop.
What will I find in my alphabet soup?
A, B, C . . .
(*When you miss, make up something that starts with the letter you missed on.*)

A my name is Alice
And my husband's name is Arthur,
We come from Alabama,
Where we sell artichokes.
B my name is Barney
And my wife's name is Bridget,
We come from Brooklyn,
Where we sell bicycles.
C my name is _____
And my husband's name is _____,
We come from _____
Where we sell _____.
(*Continue throughout the alphabet.*)

All in together, girls.
How do you like the weather, girls?
January, February, March, April . . .

Apartment for rent, inquire within,
When _____ moves out, let _____ in.
(*As one jumper jumps out, the next jumps in.*)

Apples, peaches, pears, and plums
Tell me when your birthday comes.
January, February . . .

As I went down to my grandfather's farm,
A billy goat chased me around the barn.
It chased me up a sycamore tree,
And this is what it said to me:
I like coffee, I like tea,
I like _____ to jump with me.
(*The named jumper jumps into the rope.*)

Benjamin Franklin went to France
To teach the ladies how to dance.
First the heel, and then the toe,
Spin around and out you go.
(*Follow the directions in the rhyme.*)

Bubble gum, bubble gum, chew and blow,
Bubble gum, bubble gum, scrape your toe,
Bubble gum, bubble gum, tastes so sweet,
Get that bubble gum off your feet!
(*Follow the directions in the rhyme.*)

Butterfly, Butterfly, throws a kiss, kiss, kiss,
Butterfly, Butterfly, get out before you miss, miss, miss.

Cinderella dressed in yella,
Went downstairs to kiss a fella,
Made a mistake and kissed a snake.
How many doctors did it take
1, 2, 3 . . .

Cinderella dressed in yellow
Went downstairs to kiss her fellow.
How many kisses did she give?
1, 2, 3, 4, 5 . . .

Down in the valley where the green grass grows,
There sat _____ as pretty as a rose.
She sang so high, she sang so sweet,
Along came _____ and kissed her on the cheek.
How many kisses did she get?
1, 2, 3 . . .

Grace, Grace, dressed in lace
Went upstairs to powder her face.
How many boxes did it take?
1, 2, 3 . . .

Hello, hello, hello, sir.
Meet me at the grocer.
No, sir. Why, sir?
Because I have a cold, sir.
Where did you get the cold, sir?
At the North Pole, sir.
What were you doing there, sir?
Counting polar bears, sir.
How many did you count, sir?
1, 2, 3, 4, 5 . . .

Hickety Pickety Pop,
How many times before I stop?
1, 2, 3 . . .

How do you spell Mississippi?
M (*cross arms over chest*)
I (*point to your eye*)
Crooked letter (*cross legs and jump*)
Crooked letter (*cross legs and jump*)
I (point to eye)
Crooked letter (*cross legs and jump*)
Crooked letter (*cross legs and jump*)
I (*point to eye*)
P (*hunch back*)
P (*hunch back*)
I!

I know a boy and he is doubled-jointed,
He gave me a kiss and I was disappointed.
He gave me another to match the other,
Now, now, _____, I'll tell your mother.
How many kisses did I get last night?
1, 2, 3 . . .

I like coffee,
I like tea.
I like _____ to jump with me.
(*The named jumper jumps in the rope.*)

I love coffee,
I love tea.
I love the boys
And the boys love me.

I made a wish jumping rope,
I caught a fish jumping rope,
I gave a kiss jumping rope,
How many wishes (fishes, kisses) did I get?
1, 2, 3 . . .

I'm a little Dutch girl dressed in blue.
Here are the things I like to do:
Salute to the captain, bow to the queen,
Turn my back on the submarine.
I can do the tap dance, I can do the split,
I can do the holka polka just like this.
(*Follow the directions in the rhyme.*)

Ink, ink, a bottle of ink,
The cork fell off and you stink.
Not because you're dirty, not because you're clean,
Just because you kiss the girls behind the magazine!

Lady, lady, touch the ground,
Lady, lady, turn around.
Turn to the east, and turn to the west,
And choose the one you like the best.
Lady, lady, touch the ground,
Lady, lady, turn around.
Lady, lady, show your shoe,
Lady, lady, now skidoo!

Ladybug, Ladybug, turn around,
Ladybug, Ladybug, touch the ground.
Ladybug, Ladybug, shine your shoes,
Ladybug, Ladybug, read the news.
Ladybug, Ladybug, how old are you?
1, 2, 3, 4 . . .

Mabel, Mabel, set the table,
Just as fast as you are able.
Don't forget the salt, sugar, vinegar, mustard,
Red-hot pepper!
(*Jump as fast as possible on "red-hot pepper."*)

Old Mother Whittlehouse
Had a big fit.
First she did the merry-go-round
And then she did the split.

Policeman, policeman, do your duty,
Here comes (*name of next jumper*)
And she's a cutie;
She can jump, she can twist,
But I bet she can't do this.

Robin Hood, Robin Hood, dressed so good,
Got as many kisses as he could.
How many kisses did he get?
1, 2, 3 . . .

Spanish dancer, do the splits,
Spanish dancer, do high kicks.
Spanish dancer, click a shoe,
Spanish dancer, chooses YOU!
(*Jumper follows the directions in the rhyme, and the chosen jumper jumps in the rope.*)

Teddy bear, teddy bear, dressed in blue,
Can you do what I tell you to?
Teddy bear, teddy bear, turn around.
Teddy bear, teddy bear, touch the ground.
Teddy bear, teddy bear, do the splits.
Teddy bear, teddy bear, give a high kick.
Teddy bear, teddy bear, go upstairs.
Teddy bear, teddy bear, say your prayers.
Teddy bear, teddy bear, turn out the light.
Teddy bear, teddy bear, say good night.

Three, six, nine, the goose drank wine,
The monkey chewed tobacco on the streetcar line.
The lion choked, the monkey croaked,
And they all went to heaven in a little rowboat.
1, 2, 3 . . .

Will I marry, tell me so,
Is the answer yes or no?
Yes, no, maybe so, yes, no, maybe so . . .

157. BENEFITS OF ROPE JUMPING

➡ As a weight-bearing activity, it builds strong, dense bones

➡ Body composition (lean body mass)

➡ Cardiorespiratory endurance

➡ Flexibility

➡ Muscle strength

➡ Muscular endurance

➡ Rope jumping burns 600 to 1,000 calories per hour when jumping 120 to 140 jumps per minute

➡ Skill-related fitness benefits include:

- Agility
- Balance
- Coordination
- Power
- Speed
- Timing and rhythm

➡ Other benefits include:

- Development of creativity
- Development of social skills
- Enhancement of self image
- Enjoyment
- Inexpensive
- Easy to learn

➡ Rope skipping is used for:

- Aerobics
- Competitions (speed, freestyle, single rope, and double-dutch)
- Conditioning
- Training for sports
- Warming up for sports

158. BASIC JUMP ROPE SKILLS

The rope should be long enough to reach from the floor to the armpits when the rope is folded in half. It is suggested that beginners start out slowly.

Double Bounce

➡ Jump twice in one rotation of the rope.

Single Bounce

➡ Jump once over each rotation of the rope.

Single Sideswing

1. Put the hands together while holding the handles.
2. Swing the rope from one side of the body to the other.
3. Repeat step 1.
4. Separate hands, swing the rope down, and jump.

Jogging Step

1. Turn the rope and step over the rope with one foot.
2. On the next turn of the rope, step over the rope with the other foot.
3. Jog in place while jumping the rope.

Irish Fling

1. With the first turn of the rope, land on one foot and tap the other foot out to the side.
2. With the second turn of the rope, land on the same foot and tap the other foot out in front of the body but slightly out to the side.

3. With the third turn of the rope, land on the same foot and tap the other foot out in front of the body.
4. With the fourth turn of the rope, land on the same foot and bend the other leg so the ankle is in front of the knee.
5. Repeat on the other side.

Front Cross

1. With the first turn of the rope, jump a regular jump.
2. With the second turn of the rope, cross arms and jump through the loop that was made with the rope.

Cross-Cross

1. With the first turn of the rope, jump a regular jump.
2. Quickly uncross and cross again before jumping the rope.
3. Arms should have crossed twice in one jump.

Wounded Duck

1. Jump up in the air and land with toes pointing in.
2. Jump up and land with toes pointing out.
3. Repeat.

Front Kicks

1. With the first turn of the rope, land on both feet.
2. With the second turn of the rope, land on left foot and kick right.
3. With the third turn of the rope, land on both feet.
4. With the fourth turn of the rope, land on right foot and kick left.

Double Jump

1. Start with a single bounce.
2. Jump high into the air and turn the rope as fast as possible.
3. The rope should pass under the jumper twice before landing.

Skier

1. Jump left keeping feet together.
2. Jump right keeping feet together.
3. Move feet laterally 4 to 6 inches to each side.

Side Straddle

1. Jump to straddle position.
2. Return to basic jump.
3. Keep feet shoulder-width apart as rope passes under.

Straddle Cross

1. Jump to straddle position.
2. Jump to crossed legs.
3. Keep feet shoulder-width apart and alternate legs.

Criss-Cross

1. Cross right arm over left or cross left arm over right and jump.
2. Open rope and perform basic jump.
3. Keep handles in extended position.
4. Keep hands down low on the cross.

Heel-Toe

1. Hop on left foot, touch right heel forward.
2. Hop on left foot again, touch right toe backward.
3. Repeat on opposite side.

Toe Touch

1. Hop on left foot, touch right toe to right.
2. Hop on right foot, touch left toe to left.

Twist

1. Jump and rotate hips to right side.
2. Perform basic jump.
3. Jump and rotate hips to left.

Can-Can

1. Hop on right foot, left knee up.
2. Hop on right foot, touch left toe to side of right foot.
3. Hop on right foot, kick left leg.
4. Knee lift and kick are waist high. Repeat on opposite leg.

Side Swing Cross

1. Swing rope on right side.
2. Criss-cross (right arm crosses over left).
3. Swing rope on left side.
4. Criss-cross (left arm crosses over right).

159. CHINESE JUMP ROPE

1. Begin with the rope around the ankles of two jumpers.
2. Another jumper jumps in the rope with both feet.
3. The jumper jumps out of the rope with both legs straddling each outside rope.
4. The jumper jumps from side to side (straddling each side of the rope).
5. The jumper jumps on the rope. Then out again.
6. The jumper takes the rope and crosses it using his or her legs, so that the legs are inside of an X.
7. The jumper then has to jump out and straddle the rope.
8. The jumper is eliminated if he or she lands on the rope unintentionally.
9. The jumper is eliminated if he or she misses when trying to land on the rope.

160. HISTORICAL FACTS ABOUT LACROSSE

➡ Lacrosse is the oldest sport in North America.

➡ It was originally played by Native Americans in what are now Canada and New York.

➡ It was originally played by hundreds of players in games that lasted over several days using goals that were up to 15 miles apart.

➡ Lacrosse games were originally used to toughen braves for actual combat.

➡ There were even times when games were played between two tribes to settle their differences or disputes.

➡ The game got its name because French missionaries thought the stick resembled a bishop's crozier (la crosse).

➡ The first lacrosse club was founded in Montreal in 1842.

➡ Standard rules for play were established by 1860.

➡ Lacrosse was first played in Olympic competition in the early 1900s, and the United States Intercollegiate Lacrosse League (USILL) was formed.

➡ The United States Intercollegiate Lacrosse Association replaced the USILL in 1926, and is still the governing body of lacrosse today.

161. MEN'S LACROSSE FIELD POSITIONS

Attack
➡ The attacker's responsibility is to score goals.
➡ He generally restricts his play to the offensive end.

Midfield
➡ The midfielder's responsibility is to cover the entire field playing both offense and defense.

Defense
➡ The defender's responsibility is to defend the goal.
➡ He generally restricts his play to the defensive end of the field.

Goal
➡ The goalie's responsibility is to protect the goal and stop the opposing team from scoring.

162. BASIC RULES OF MEN'S LACROSSE

➡ Men's lacrosse is a contact game played by ten players: a goalkeeper, three defenders, three midfielders, and three attackers.

➡ The object of the game is to shoot the ball into the opponent's goal.

➡ The team scoring more goals wins.

➡ Each team must keep at least four players, including the goalie, in its defensive half of the field and three in its offensive half.

➡ Three players (midfielders) may roam the entire field.

➡ High school games are generally 48 minutes long, with 12-minute quarters.

➡ Each team is given a 2-minute break between the first and second quarters, and the third and fourth quarters.

➡ Half time is ten minutes long.

➡ Teams change sides between periods.

➡ Each team is permitted two timeouts each half.

➡ The team winning the coin toss chooses the end of the field it wants to defend first.

➡ Men's lacrosse begins with a face-off.

➡ The ball is placed between the sticks of two squatting players at the center of the field.

➡ The official blows the whistle to begin play.

➡ Each face-off player tries to control the ball.

➡ The players in the wing areas can release; the other players must wait until one player has gained possession of the ball or the ball has crossed the goal line.

➡ Center face-offs are also used after a goal and at the start of each quarter.

➡ Players may run with the ball in the crosse, pass, and catch the ball.

➡ Only the goalkeeper may touch the ball with his hands.

➡ A player may gain possession of the ball by dislodging it from an opponent's crosse with a stick check, which includes the controlled poking and slapping of the stick and gloved hands of the player in possession of the ball.

➡ Body checking is permitted if the opponent has the ball.

➡ All body contact must occur from the front or side, above the waist, and below the shoulders.

➡ An opponent's crosse may be stick-checked if it is within five yards of a loose ball or ball in the air.

➡ If the ball or a player in possession of the ball goes out of bounds, the other team is awarded possession of the ball.

➡ If the ball goes out of bounds after an unsuccessful shot on goal, the player nearest to the ball when and where it goes out of bounds is awarded possession.

➡ An attacking player cannot enter the crease around the goal, but may reach in with his stick to scoop a loose ball.

163. PERSONAL FOULS IN MEN'S LACROSSE

The penalty for a personal foul is a 1- to 3-minute suspension from play and possession to the team that was fouled. Players with five personal fouls are ejected from the game.

Slashing	A player's stick contacts an opponent in any area other than the stick or gloved hand on the stick.
Tripping	A player obstructs his opponent at or below the waist with the crosse, hands, arms, feet, or legs.
Cross Checking	A player uses the handle of his crosse to make contact with an opponent.
Unsportsmanlike Conduct	Any player or coach commits an act that is considered unsportsmanlike by an official, including taunting, obscene language or gestures, and arguing.
Unnecessary Roughness	A player strikes an opponent with his stick or body using excessive or violent force.
Illegal Crosse	A player uses a crosse that does not conform to required specifications. A crosse may be found illegal if the pocket is too deep or if the crosse was altered to gain an advantage.
Illegal Body Checking	Occurs when any of the following actions take place:

- Body checking of an opponent who is not in possession of the ball or within five yards of a loose ball.
- Avoidable body check of an opponent after he has passed or shot the ball.
- Body checking of an opponent from the rear or at or below the waist.
- Body checking of an opponent by a player in which contact is made above the shoulders of the opponent. A body check must be below the neck, and both hands of the player applying the body check must remain in contact with his crosse.

Illegal Gloves	A player uses gloves that do not conform to required specifications. A glove will be found illegal if the fingers and palms are cut out of the gloves, or if the glove has been altered in a way that compromises its protective features.

164. TECHNICAL FOULS IN MEN'S LACROSSE

The penalty for a technical foul is a 30-second suspension if a team is in possession of the ball when the foul is committed or possession of the ball to the team that was fouled if there was no possession when the foul was committed.

Holding A player impedes the movement of an opponent or an opponent's crosse.

Interference A player interferes in any manner with the free movement of an opponent, except when that opponent has possession of the ball, the ball is in flight and within five yards of the players, or both players are within five yards of a loose ball.

Offsides A team does not have at least four players on its defensive side of the midfield line or at least three players on its offensive side of the midfield line.

Pushing A player thrusts or shoves a player from behind.

Screening An offensive player illegally moves into and makes contact with a defensive player with the purpose of blocking him from the man he is defending.

Stalling A team intentionally holds the ball without conducting normal offensive play, with the intent of running time off the clock.

Warding Off A player in possession of the ball uses his free hand or arm to hold, push, or control the direction of an opponent's stick check.

165. LACROSSE PLAYING FIELD

Although women's lacrosse fields have no boundaries, an area of 120 yards × 70 yards is desirable. For men's lacrosse, the dimensions are as follows: width: 60 yards; wing area to sideline: 10 yards; wing area to center spot: 20 yards; center line to goal area line: 20 yards.

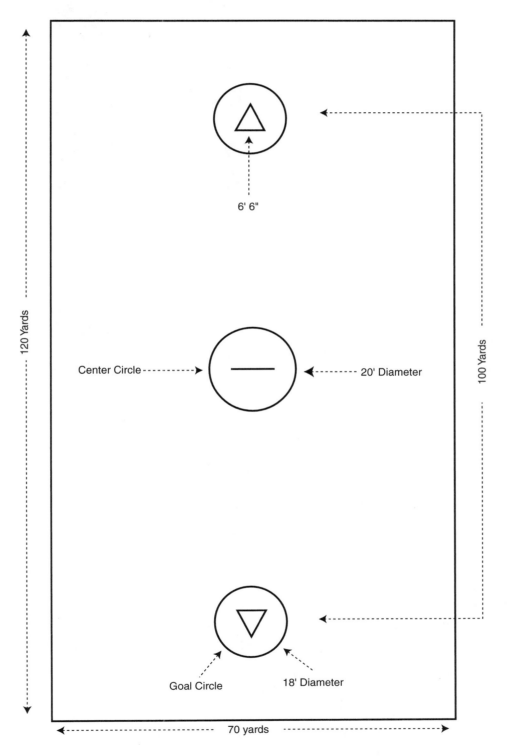

166. WOMEN'S LACROSSE FIELD POSITIONS

There are 12 players on each team, including the goalie.

Attack Positions

➡ Center

➡ Right Attack Wing

➡ Left Attack Wing

➡ Third Home

➡ Second Home

➡ First Home

Defense Positions

➡ Right Defense Wing

➡ Left Defense Wing

➡ Third Man

➡ Cover Point

➡ Point

➡ Goalie

167. BASIC RULES OF WOMEN'S LACROSSE

➡ A game begins when the two centers from each team *draw* at the center of the field: a ball is placed between their two sticks pressed together back-to-back.

➡ When the umpire calls "draw," the centers attempt to control the ball when they push the ball up and out of the circle.

➡ When a team attains control, players run and pass the ball to push it downfield toward the goal.

➡ *Cradling* is the method by which a player holds the ball in the stick's pocket.

➡ Unlike men's lacrosse, women's sticks may not have a deep pocket in which to hold the ball securely; a player cradles the ball to keep it in the pocket.

➡ Cradling uses centripetal force to press the ball into the back of the pocket.

➡ When a player has an opening to the goal, she shoots the ball by pushing the head of the stick forward and pulling the shaft back.

➡ Passing is the fastest way to get the ball downfield.

➡ Catching the pass involves having the ball land in your stick and putting it immediately into a cradle to gain control of the ball and prevent yourself from being checked.

➡ *Checking* is the technique in which a series of short, sharp, controlled strikes to an opponent's stick is used to force a player carrying the ball to drop it.

➡ A player can check the head or shaft of the stick, or body check.

➡ Body checking is accomplished when a defender sticks close to her opponent in an effort to intimidate the player into dropping the ball, or changing the opponent's path towards the goal.

➡ If a player commits a minor foul, she must forfeit possession of the ball (if she has it) and move four meters either to the side or in front of the player whom she fouled.

➡ If a player commits a major foul, she must forfeit possession of the ball (if she has it) and move four meters behind the player whom she fouled.

➡ If a major foul is committed in the arc by the defense, a "free shot" on goal is taken by the player fouled.

➡ All of the defense players are required to clear the arc to the border closest to which they were standing when the whistle blew.

➡ The attack player who was fouled takes her place at the hash mark closest to which she was standing when she was fouled.

➡ The defense must move away at least four meters from the fouled player.

➡ When the umpire blows the whistle again, the player can take a shot on goal or pass while the defense moves in.

➡ There are no boundaries to the field, but if a ball enters an area that is dangerous, unplayable, or not clearly visible to the umpire, the player who retains it or is closest to it (if the ball has been grounded) at the umpire's whistle wins it.

➡ The player then waits for the second whistle to begin play again, either by running with or passing the ball.

➡ When the umpire blows the whistle because a foul has occurred, or the ball has gone "out of bounds," all players must stop and check all forward movement.

➡ Play resumes and the players can move when the umpire blows the whistle again.

➡ Checking (the method by which a player knocks the ball from an opponent's stick) is prohibited:
  • When it is directed toward the face
  • When it is uncontrolled
  • When it holds down the other's stick
  • When the checker's stick is too close to the head or face

➡ Defenders may not remain in the arc without guarding another player.

➡ When the ball is grounded, covering it with the back of a stick's net and preventing play by another player is prohibited.

➡ No players, other than the goalie, may enter the circle around the goal cage.

➡ When a foul occurs, the player who was fouled is allowed a free shot at the goal, with the defense pushed to the perimeter around the arc.

168. HISTORICAL FACTS ABOUT PADDLEBALL

➡ Irish immigrants brought a game called handball to America in the 1850s.

➡ Due to the cold weather in upstate New York, the players carved wooden paddles to hit the ball with in order to relieve the hand pain from the cold, hard balls.

➡ Dr. Frank Beale of Brooklyn, New York developed the *paddlestick* design.

169. PADDLEBALL PADDLE AND BALLS

➡ The paddle can be no longer than 18 inches from the edge of its face to the edge of the handle.

➡ The face cannot be wider than 9 inches.

➡ The paddle cannot have any stringing such as a tennis racquet.

➡ The ball should be made of rubber with a $1\frac{7}{8}$-inch diameter with a $\frac{1}{32}$-inch in variance.

➡ The weight should be $2\frac{3}{10}$ ounces with a $\frac{2}{10}$-ounce variance.

➡ The ball should rebound 44 to 52 inches from a 70-inch drop at 68 degrees Fahrenheit.

170. PADDLEBALL SAFETY RULES

➡ It is each player's obligation to exercise caution when swinging a paddle, and not to hit any player on the court.

➡ When the hitter unintentionally causes contact with the backward motion of the swing with his or her opponent, play will stop and the volley will be replayed.

➡ Moving into the swing of another player is an out.

➡ If a hitter makes contact with his or her opponent in the course of a normal follow-through, either the volley will continue because neither player reacted significantly to the contact, or the volley will be stopped and an out will be charged against the hitter.

➡ When a ball rolls into another court, players must wait until the play is stopped before attempting to retrieve the ball.

171. PADDLEBALL COURT

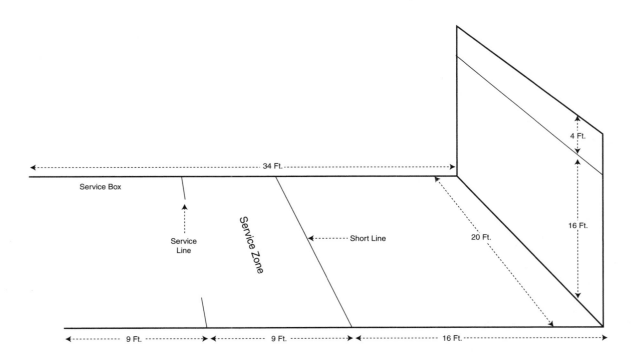

172. BASIC RULES FOR ONE-WALL PADDLEBALL

One-wall paddleball is a game played by two teams in which a ball is hit by a paddle against a wall in such a manner that it creates an exchange or volley between the two teams. Each point or volley is begun with the ball being served against the wall. The volleying continues back and forth until one team fails to return the ball in accordance with the rules. Each team must hit the ball in consecutive order. Any member on the team can hit for the team.

General Rules

➡ There may be two players on the court for singles or four on the court for doubles. An even number of players must be on a team.

➡ Game is over when one team is the first to score the required amount of points (11, 15, 21, or 25) by a 2-point margin.

➡ Points can only be awarded to the serving team and are scored when the receiving team makes an out.

➡ A legally played ball is one that is struck in the proper order by the players on a fly or one bounce.

➡ The ball must bounce both in the playing area of the wall and the floor.

➡ The order of hitting the ball must be constant during the volley.

➡ Any team that makes contact with the ball out of order will be out.

➡ The order alternates from one team to the other.

➡ A team that is struck with its returned ball will be out, except when a ball rebounds off the wall and passes both opponents, who have no chance to return the ball, and the ball hits one of the hitting team without bouncing.

➡ If the ball was determined to bounce out, the hitting team is out. If the ball was determined to bounce fair, the volley has been won by the hitting team. If the ball passes both opponents, with no chance of returning the ball, bounces and hits the hitting team, then the hitting team wins the volley. (A reasonable attempt must be made to return the ball in play.)

➡ A team may swing and miss any number of times at the ball until it has bounced twice.

➡ The hand (that is holding the paddle) from the wrist down is part of the paddle and is legal contact area.

➡ The paddle may be switched from one hand to the other.

➡ If a player's paddle is dislodged from his or her hand, the player is out.

➡ Should a player's paddle be dislodged accidentally by his or her opponent, the volley will be replayed.

➡ Once a ball is served, no appeal can be requested for a prior play.

Timeouts

➡ 15-point game: two 1-minute timeouts

➡ 21- and 25-point games: three 1-minute timeouts

➡ 10-second timeouts may be requested by a player for wiping hands, cleaning glasses, tying shoelaces, etc.

Service

A coin is tossed to determine which team will serve first. The winning team of the toss elects whether to serve or receive.

Legal Serve	The ball is required to hit inbound on the wall first and rebound into the service and receiving area.
Short Serve	The ball hits inbound on the wall and rebounds into the short service area. The ball is a legal serve if it bounces on the short line.
Long Serve	The ball hits inbound on the wall and rebounds into the long area. The ball is a legal serve if it bounces on the long line.
Service Release Bounces	The server must serve the ball on one bounce. The ball must bounce in the service area.
Service Miss	If the server swings at the ball and misses it, the server is out.
Service Position	The server must start and finish within the service area when in the act of serving.
Illegal Service Moving	The server's team cannot step backward into the receiving area until the receiving team hits the ball, and the receiving team cannot step forward into the service area until after they hit the ball.
Paddle Position	The server's paddle is allowed to extend over the short line and the right or left boundary lines. The server's paddle is not allowed to extend over the service markers. The receiving team's paddle may not extend past the service markers.
Screened Serve	A screened serve happens when the server must move his or her body to let the ball pass after it rebounds off the wall. A screened serve is replayed.
Hit with the Served Ball	If a served ball hits either of the serving team's members, the server is out. If the served ball hits the receiving team on a fly, then it is a point.

Doubles Serve

If the team winning the coin toss elects to serve first, then they have one serve for their first set of serves. If the team winning the coin toss declines the first serve, then the opposing team will have two serves for their first set of serves. From that point on, both teams will have two serves apiece.

➡ Each team has two serves and two faults.

➡ Each team member must serve.

➡ Serving is in successive order (one after the other).

➡ The first server on a team will serve until his or her team makes one out.

➡ The second server on the team will serve until his or her team makes a second out.

➡ Then the side will be retired and the opposing team will serve.

➡ The server's partner must stand off the court, between the extensions of the short line and the service marker, during the serve.

➡ The nonserving partner's feet are not to be positioned on any of the boundary lines or service markers.

➡ The server's partner may enter the court area after the ball passes.

➡ The server's served ball may not pass between the legs or the legs of his or her partner.

➡ The server may serve from any position in the service area, and serve the ball on either side of his or her body.

Singles Serve

➡ Each team has one serve, and one fault is equal to an out.

➡ The position of the server's feet from start to finish of his or her serves divides the court into the Major Service Area—Minor Service Area—Automatic Fault Area.

➡ *Automatic Fault Area* is determined by the position of the server's right foot and left foot at the conclusion of serving. Imaginary lines are drawn parallel to the boundary lines from the wall to the long line and the width is determined by the right and left feet. During the serve, the ball may not bounce into this area.

➡ *Major Service Area* is the larger of the two remaining service areas, and is the area where the ball will be served into except when the server designates to serve into the Minor Service Area.

➡ *Minor Service Area* is the smaller of the two remaining service areas. The server must announce to the opponent before serving into the Minor Service Area.

➡ If the server creates two equal serving areas, both will be minor serving areas.

Receiving Service

➡ The receiving team may stand anywhere behind the service markers, on or off the court.

➡ The receiving team must make contact with the ball, and complete the follow-through swing before crossing the service marker with their body or paddle.

➡ The receiving team must allow a long served ball to bounce in the long area in order for a long fault to be charged to the server. If any contact by the receiving team's paddle or body is made with the ball before it bounces long, it will be considered a ball in play.

➡ A served fly ball that the receiving team swings at and misses, which bounces in the long area or out of the boundary lines will be a long fault or server out, respectively.

Illegal Movement

➡ *Illegal movement* is when a player on either team moves in a manner that gives him or her an advantage by causing interference with the opponent's ability to play, see, or move to the ball.

➡ *Crossing the ball* is when a player crosses the path of the ball that is rebounding from the wall. An exception is when a player hits the ball and the rebounding shot from the wall is traveling directly at him or her. The player may then move to either the right or left regardless if he or she moves into the swing of the hitter.

Faults

➡ Two consecutive faults will be an out.

Outs or Points

➡ *Outside ball* is any ball bouncing outside the boundary lines (wall and floor) and past the long line. It is an out or a point.

➡ *Ball hitting under* is any ball that hits the floor first on its trajectory towards the wall. It will be an underhit ball and is an out or a point.

➡ A player will be called out if he or she purposely hits his or her opponent(s) with the ball.

173. HISTORICAL FACTS ABOUT PADDLE TENNIS

→ The game of paddle tennis originated in 1898 as a game for children.

→ Reverend Frank P. Beals of Albion, Michigan invented it for children too young to play lawn tennis.

→ The original court was 18 feet by 39 feet.

→ The game was brought to New York City when Reverend Beals's ministry was transferred to Greenwich Village.

→ The U.S. Paddle Tennis Association was formed in 1926.

→ Murray Geller completely revised the rules and court markings and dimensions in 1959.

174. PADDLE TENNIS BALL AND PADDLE

BALL

The ball should be a pressurized tennis ball, approved by the United States Tennis Association, which has its internal pressure reduced by being punctured so that when dropped from a height of six feet to the playing court surface, the bounce will be not less than 31 inches nor more than 33 inches. Puncturing with a hypodermic needle or safety pin is a simple method of achieving the required bounce.

PADDLE

The paddle should be made of solid material or materials, and should be not more than 9 1/2 by 18 inches. It may be perforated and/or textured, but should contain no strings.

175. PADDLE TENNIS COURT

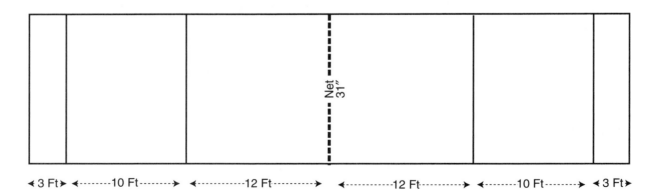

176. BASIC RULES OF PADDLE TENNIS

The Server

➡ Only one serve is allowed.

➡ The server must stand behind the base line and within the imaginary extensions of the center and side lines.

➡ The server then projects the ball by hand into the air and strikes it with the paddle at a point not higher than 31 inches above the court surface at the instant of impact; or, the server may bounce or drop the ball to the court surface behind the base line and strike it with the paddle upon its rebound at a point not higher than 31 inches above the court surface.

➡ The server may choose either method of serving, but, whichever alternative he or she chooses, he or she must continue to serve in that manner for the entire set.

➡ The serve must land within the service area on the receiver's side diagonally from where the server stands.

➡ If the serve fails to land within the correct area, or if the server strikes the ball higher than 31 inches above the court surface at the instant of impact, the serve is a fault and the server loses that point.

➡ The server's score is always called first.

➡ Service should begin in the right-hand or "deuce" court at the start of every game and should move from there to the left-hand court, alternating at each point until the game is completed.

➡ If the ball is served from the wrong court and is not detected, all points scored will stand.

➡ A fault is ruled if the server, in attempting to serve, misses the ball, or if the ball served touches a permanent fixture (other than the net, strap, or band) before hitting the ground.

➡ The service is a "let" if the ball touches the net, strap, or band, and is otherwise good; or after touching the net, strap, or band, touches a receiver or anything the receiver wears or carries; or if a serve, good or fault, is delivered when the receiver is not ready.

➡ When a let is called, the point should be replayed.

➡ At the end of the first game, the receiver becomes the server and vice versa, and so on alternately until the match is over.

➡ If a player serves out of turn, the correct player shall serve as soon as the mistake is apparent, but all points scored remain the same.

➡ Each player must allow the ball to bounce once on his or her side (exclusive of dropping the ball behind the base line) before being permitted to volley for the first time.

➡ The receiver wins the point if the serve is a fault.

A Player

A player loses the point to the opponent if:

→ He or she returns any ball after a second bounce.

→ He or she returns the ball in play so that it hits the ground, a permanent fixture, or other object outside the opponent's court.

→ He or she volleys the ball without making a good return, even if standing out of the court.

→ He or she carries, touches, or strikes the ball with his or her paddle more than once during a stroke.

→ His or her body or paddle (in his or her hand or otherwise), or anything he or she is wearing or carrying, touches the net, posts, cord or metal cable, strap or band, or the ground within the opponent's court at anytime while the ball is in play.

→ He or she volleys a ball before it has crossed the net.

→ The ball in play touches a player or anything he or she is wearing or carrying, except his or her paddle or glove, or hands holding onto the paddle.

→ He or she throws the paddle and hits the ball.

→ He or she hits a ball in the gap between the net and post and lower than the net cord. It is a "pass through" ball and the player loses the point, even though the ball lands in the proper court.

→ His or her momentum causes his or her body or paddle or anything he or she is wearing or carrying to contact the net, posts, cord or metal cable, strap, or band.

→ He or she strikes the ball with his or her paddle during service at a point higher than 31 inches above the court surface.

→ He or she returns a ball that hits a permanent fixture before hitting the ground.

→ The paddles of both partners strike the ball in play during one stroke in doubles play.

→ The server hits the return of service as a volley in singles play.

→ A player footfaults during service delivery.

→ A served ball touches the server's partner.

→ He or she deliberately hinders the opponent from making a stroke.

→ He or she footfaults by standing out of the designated area.

→ He or she misses the ball while attempting to serve, or the served ball touches a permanent fixture before hitting the ground.

→ In serving, he or she drops the ball in front of the base line.

→ He or she hits a ball that hits that part of the net post that protrudes above the net.

→ If he or she deliberately hinders his opponent from making a stroke, the point is awarded to the opponent; or if involuntary, the point will be replayed.

184. SHUFFLEBOARD COURT

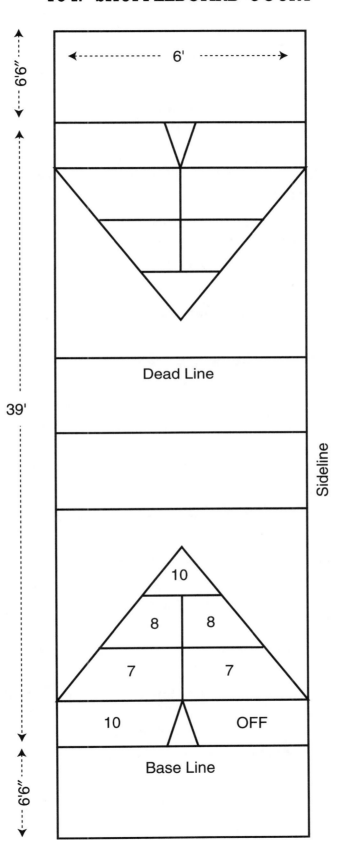

185. BASIC RULES OF SHUFFLEBOARD

→ Shuffleboard may be played as singles or doubles.

→ A coin is tossed to determine choice of color.

→ To start a game, the *red* disc is shot first.

→ Play alternates (red, then black) until all discs are shot.

→ Red should always be played from the right side of the *head of court*, and left side of *foot of court*.

→ In singles, after all discs are played (a half round), the players walk to the opposite end of the court and start play.

→ In doubles, after all discs are played at *head of court*, play starts at *foot* or opposite end—red leading, black following.

→ Color lead does not change until both ends have been played (*a round*).

→ Game is played to 50, 75, or 100 points.

→ Players must place their four discs within and not touching the lines of their respective half of the *10 off* area.

→ The penalty is 5 points off and is not applied to a player until he or she has played a disc.

→ If disc played touches the front or back lines, the penalty is 5 off.

→ If disc played touches sideline or triangle, the penalty is 10 off, the offender's disc is removed, and the opponent is credited with any disc displaced.

→ All displaced discs shall be removed from the court immediately after scoring of the opponent's displaced discs.

→ No penalty is imposed if the disc being played should touch or cross the separation triangle.

→ Discs may be moved and played from any spot within the respective 10 off area.

→ The forward motion of cue and disc must be continuous or the penalty is 10 off, the offender's disc removed, and the opponent is credited with score of any of the discs displaced.

→ All displaced discs must be removed from the court immediately after the scoring of the opponent's displaced discs.

→ The shot must be delivered in a straight line with a continuous forward motion of cue and disc or a 10 off penalty is imposed, the offender's disc is removed, and the opponent is credited with score of any discs displaced.

→ All displaced discs must be removed from the court immediately after scoring of opponent's displaced discs.

➡ Players may not step on or over base line of court, or extension of base line, except to gather and place their discs.

➡ There is a 5-point penalty for this offense when not in the act of executing a shot.

➡ Players must not touch a foot, hand, knee, or any other part of their body to the court on or over the base line or extension of the base line at any time while executing a shot, or incur a penalty of 10 points.

➡ Players may not stand in the way of, or have a cue in the way of, or interfere with opponent while he or she is executing a play, or incur a 5-point penalty.

➡ Players may not touch live discs at any time without incurring a 5-point penalty.

➡ A disc or discs returning or remaining on the playing area of the court, after having struck any object outside the playing area (dead disc), shall be removed before further play.

➡ If a dead disc rebounds and touches a live disc, or causes another dead disc to touch a live disc, the half-round must be played over. The exception is if it was the result of the last disc, which is the eighth disc, played in the half-round; then the half-round is not replayed, and any score that was on the board immediately before the rebound counts.

➡ If a dead disc coming from another court moves or displaces a live disc, that half-round shall be played over, with no score credited to any player.

➡ A disc that stops in an area between farthest dead line and starting area is dead, and must be removed before further play. If the disc is touching the farthest dead line, it is in play.

➡ Any disc that clearly leaves the court beyond the farthest base line or goes off the sides of the court is a dead disc.

➡ A disc that stops less than eight inches beyond the farthest base line should be removed.

➡ A disc that is leaning over the edge of the court and touching the alley must be immediately removed.

➡ Players shooting before an opponent's disc comes to rest incur a penalty of 10 points, the offender's disc is removed, and the opponent is credited with any discs displaced.

➡ All displaced discs shall be removed from the court immediately after scoring of opponent's displaced discs.

➡ If a cue slips from a player's hand and touches or displaces any live disc, the player is penalized 10 points and the opponent is credited with any of his or her discs displaced, and that half-round must be played over unless game point has been reached.

186. SHUFFLEBOARD SCORING INSTRUCTIONS

➡ The score sheet includes one 10-point area, two 8-point areas, two 7-point areas, and one 10-off area.

➡ After both players have shot their four discs, *all* discs on the diagram within and not touching lines should be scored. (The separation triangle in 10-off area is not considered.)

➡ When judging discs in relation to lines, the player or official should sight *directly down*.

➡ Play continues until all discs have been shot in that half-round, even if game point has been reached.

➡ If a tie game results at game point or over, play is continued in regular rotation of play until two full rounds in doubles or one full round in singles are completed. At that time the side with the higher score wins, even if it has less than 75 points or the number of points specified as game points. If the score is tied again, play continues again as described.

194. HISTORICAL FACTS ABOUT SOFTBALL

➡ Softball was invented around the beginning of the twentieth century by American professional baseball players who wanted to keep in practice during the off-season late fall and winter months. The substitute game was played indoors.

➡ Different variations were played under the names of "Diamond Ball," "Kitten Ball," "Mush Ball," "Pumpkin Ball," and "Recreation Ball."

➡ The first softball league was organized in Minnesota in 1900 and the game was officially named *Softball* in 1926.

➡ Toward the end of the 1920s, Canadian amateur players began to play the new game outdoors on playgrounds or other suitable fields. The game then rapidly became popular in Canada and obtained a foothold in the United States.

➡ Extensive interest in softball began in the United States about 1930. The first national amateur softball tournament took place in Chicago, Illinois in 1933 in connection with the World's Fair then being held in that city. After about 20 years, when fast pitching began to dominate the game, slow-pitch softball was developed in order to give batters a better chance at hitting the ball. The popularity of slow-pitch softball spread abroad, especially in Mexico, Cuba, Japan, and Australia.

➡ The Amateur Softball Association (ASA) was founded in 1933 to standardize the rules and govern the sport. It is still the governing body for softball in the United States.

➡ During World War II, American servicemen played the game wherever they were stationed, introducing softball to other countries.

➡ Under the ASA, annual sectional tournaments for both fast-pitch and slow-pitch softball are held for men and women. The winners of these tournaments and the championship team of the previous year meet in national championship tournaments. The first World Softball Championship was played in 1966.

➡ In 1991 women's fast-pitch softball was selected to debut as an event at the 1996 Olympic Games in Atlanta, Georgia.

195. SOFTBALL EQUIPMENT

Bat

➡ The bat must be made of one piece of wood (hardwood), or laminated wood sections, metal, plastic, bamboo, or a combination of materials.

➡ It should be smooth and round with a maximum diameter of 2 1/4 inches. The bat may not be more than 34 inches in length, and no more than 38 ounces in weight.

➡ The bat should have a safety grip of cork, tape (not smooth plastic type), or combination material. The grip shall not be less than 10 inches long and shall not extend more than 15 inches from the small end of the bat.

➡ The bat shall be marked "OFFICIAL SOFTBALL" by the manufacturer.

Ball

➡ The ball is smooth seamed and concealed stitched, or flat surfaced, and made of stitched horsehide or cowhide or a molded synthetic cover over a kapok, rubber, cork, or poly-mix center core.

➡ The ball is 12 inches in diameter. The youth division (boys and girls 10 and under) often uses the 11-inch softball.

➡ The ball weighs $6^{1}/_{4}$ to 7 ounces.

Gloves or Mitts

➡ All fielders must wear gloves or mitts made of leather.

➡ Only the catcher and first baseman may wear mitts.

➡ Gloves or mitts with white or gray circles on the outside, giving the appearance of a ball, may not be worn by any player and will be considered illegal.

➡ Webbing may not be more than 5 inches long.

196. SOFTBALL FIELDING POSITIONS

Pitcher

➡ The pitcher is the person who pitches the ball.

➡ Once the ball has been pitched, the pitcher should be prepared for the ball to be hit back at him or her.

➡ The pitcher also backs up the majority of the bases (stands about five feet behind the base player when a throw is coming in).

Catcher

➡ The catcher is the person who receives the pitch if the ball is not hit.

➡ The catcher is responsible for any force plays or tags at home plate.

First Base

➡ The first base player fields about six feet away from first base until the ball is hit.

➡ Once the ball is hit, if the ball is hit away from first base, the first base player needs to take the base and be ready to receive the throw.

➡ If the ball is hit to the outfield and there will be no play to first, the first base player should not take the base, since doing so will only impede the runner and be dangerous.

➡ The general rule for any base player is "ball before base." If the ball is hit in first base's direction, first should get the ball and let someone else (usually pitcher) get the base. If the throw is nowhere near the base, the first base player should step off the base and take the ball, since anything going past first base will generally be an overthrow, dead ball, and two-base award.

Second Base

➡ The second base player fields about halfway down the line, *not* next to the base.

➡ The second base player is responsible for second base if the ball is hit left.

➡ If the ball is hit right, the second base player tries to field the ball while the shortstop takes second base.

➡ The second base player takes the cut to any outfield hits to right field.

Third Base

➡ The third base player is responsible for third base and balls that he or she can field.

Shortstop

→ The shortstop is responsible for the area not covered by third base on the left side of the infield.

→ The shortstop is in charge on the infield and controls the team by calling the plays.

→ The shortstop takes the cuts for outfield hits to the left side of the field.

→ The shortstop takes second base if the ball is hit to the right and the second base player is fielding the ball or going for the cut.

Left Fielder

→ This outfielder generally takes care of most of the left side of the outfield.

→ If necessary, the left fielder might come towards the infield to cover third base.

→ The left fielder also covers any fly balls hit to left center.

Center Fielder

→ This player stands in the center left and covers the potential infield errors where possible.

→ The center fielder covers any fly balls hit to left field or center right.

Right Fielder

→ This player stands in center right and covers the throws to second base.

→ The right fielder covers any fly balls hit to center left or right field.

Extra Fielder (Slow Pitch)

→ This player stands in right field and, if in close enough, might decide to cover the throws to first.

→ This player also covers any fly balls hit to center right.

Additional Players

→ In *fast pitch,* a **designated player (DP)** who is named before the game may bat for another team member, but must keep the same place in the batting order for the entire game. The designated player may play defense, but the starting player and the designated player may not be in the game at the same time.

→ In *slow pitch,* an **extra player (EP)** named before the game may play as a batter but must play the entire game. All 11 players can interchange positions.

→ All starting players, including DPs and EPs, may be substituted for and can reenter the game one time but must bat in their original place. If substitutes are replaced, they may not reenter.

197. SOFTBALL FIELD DIAGRAM

The regulation softball field distances vary for fast and slow pitch softball and for males and females. Base paths measure 60 feet for fast pitch and 65 feet for slow pitch for males, but 60 feet for fast and slow pitch for females. The pitching distance measures 46 feet for both fast and slow pitch for males and for slow pitch for females, but only 40 feet for fast pitch for females.

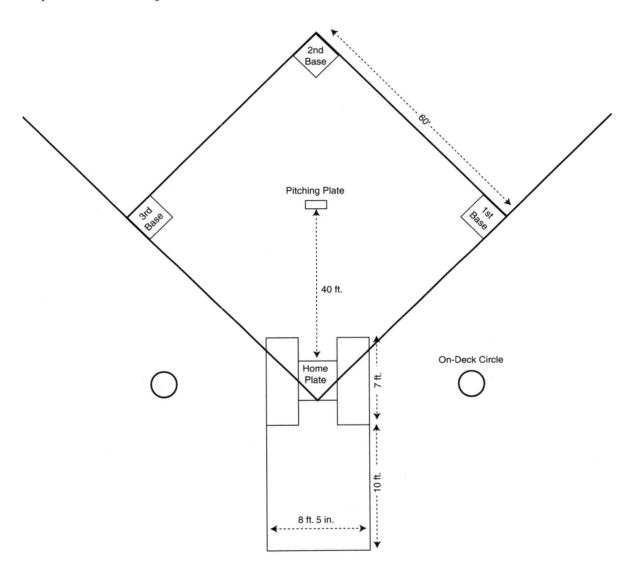

198. BASIC SOFTBALL RULES

Softball is a sport similar to baseball. The same basic equipment is used, except the ball is slightly larger, the playing field is slightly smaller, and the ball is pitched underhand. A regulation game is seven innings long. There are two types of softball: fast pitch and slow pitch. Fast pitch is played with 9 members, while slow pitch uses 10, adding a short fielder. In slow pitch, the ball is pitched in a high, slow arc, making it an easy target to hit, usually resulting in high scoring games. Fast-pitch games are usually low scoring games, and emphasis is placed more on pitching. In slow pitch, bunting and base stealing are not allowed. Aluminum bats are also widely used.

General Rules

➡ In the game of softball, as in baseball, two teams take turns playing in the field and at bat for an established number of innings, with the home team batting last.

➡ The players on the team bat in a specified order (batting order).

➡ The batter, using a bat, tries to hit the ball delivered by the opposing team's pitcher.

➡ The pitcher tries to vary the speed and placement of the ball within the batter's strike zone (area over home plate between the batter's knees and armpits).

➡ Each team is allowed three outs when at bat.

➡ An out can occur several ways:

- A ball is caught before touching the ground
- A ground ball is caught and thrown to first base before the batter gets there
- A baserunner is not touching a base and is tagged by a fielder holding the ball
- A fielder holding a ball touches a base with a runner advancing to it, and runners are on the previous bases
- A player leaves a base and does not get back before a caught fly ball is thrown to that base when the pitcher gets three strikes on the batter

➡ A strike is a ball swung at and missed, a ball hit into foul territory (except on the third strike), or a ball not swung at but within the strike zone.

➡ The team at bat tries to get runners on the bases and advance them around all the bases to score runs.

➡ The team with more runs after seven innings is the winner.

➡ The most common way of getting on base is with a hit.

➡ On a hit, the batter and runners try to advance as far as possible.

➡ If a batter advances to only first base, it is called a single; to second base on one hit, a double; to third base on one hit, a triple; and all the way around the bases on one hit, a homerun.

➡ A homerun may also be any ball hit on the fly and in fair territory that goes over the fence or wall in the outfield.

➡ Batters may also advance to first base if hit by a pitched ball, or by receiving a walk (not swinging at four pitches outside the strike zone).

➡ Another way runners may advance to a base is by stealing.

Batting

➡ When batting, both feet must remain in the batter's box until the ball has been hit. Failing to do so results in the batter being called out.

➡ Each batter gets four balls and three strikes (a ball being a bad pitch, a strike being a good one).

➡ If a batter swings for the pitch, it will be called a strike, regardless of whether it was a ball or strike.

➡ The batters must bat in the same order.

➡ The on-deck batter (batter waiting to hit) must not enter the batting box or the field of play until the play resulting from the previous batter has finished.

Pitching

➡ The pitcher must begin the pitch with one foot on the pitching plate.

➡ The pitcher must remain in contact with the pitching plate until the pitch has been released.

➡ The pitch must reach an arc of between 6 to 12 feet from the ground in slow-pitch softball.

➡ For a pitch to be called a strike, it must be between 6 to 12 feet at its peak and cross the home plate between the batter's front knee and back shoulder. Anything else will be called a ball.

➡ Any type of windup is permitted, but once the pitcher has begun the motion, he or she may not stop or reverse.

➡ The windmill motion is not permitted in slow-pitch softball.

Baserunning

➡ Once the batter reaches first base, he or she is called a baserunner.

➡ A player is not obliged to go around all the bases at once to score.

➡ Any runner passing home will score, even if he or she has stopped on every single base.

➡ A player must touch every base as he or she goes around.

➡ The baserunner must not deviate from his or her natural running path to avoid a tag; doing so results in the baserunner being called out.

➡ If the ball is caught off the bat and the baserunner has left the base she or he was occupying, he or she must return to that base before attempting to proceed (tagging up).

Fielding

→ When the fielding side makes three outs, the teams switch over.

→ To force a runner out at a base, the runner must be forced to the next base. For example, the batter is forced to run to first base when that runner hits the ball and if there is anyone on first base, then he or she will be forced to second.

→ To force a runner out, the ball must reach the base before the runner and the base player must have control of the ball and must have some part of him- or herself touching the base.

→ To tag a runner out, all you need to do is touch the runner with the ball or the glove with the ball in it.

→ If a runner is not forced to run, he or she must be tagged in order to be called out.

→ If the ball is overthrown and goes dead, the runners are awarded two bases from the last base touched at the point of the throw.

→ The ball can be caught and an out made if the ball is hit foul.

199. SOFTBALL TERMINOLOGY

Backstop The fence behind home plate.

Bag The base.

Balk When the pitcher makes a motion to pitch the ball, but does not deliver the ball immediately. When this happens, the batter is given a ball, and the baserunners may advance one base.

Base on Balls When a batter receives four balls and may advance to first base without being called out.

Base Path An imaginary line on the playing field, extending three feet to either side of a direct line between the bases.

Bases Loaded A runner on each base.

Batter's Box The area in which the batter must stand when batting.

Batting Average Divide the total number of hits a batter has made by the total number of times at bat.

Batting Order The official order in which a team must come to bat.

Bobble Fumbling with the ball while trying to catch it.

Bunt A legally hit ball that is not swung at, but rather tapped slowly within the infield.

Catcher's Box The area the catcher must stay in when calling signals and catching the pitched ball.

Cleanup The fourth hitter in the batting order. This is usually the best hitter, and is hopefully able to bring any runners home.

Count The number of balls and strikes.

Defensive Team The team on the field.

Diamond The area formed by the home plate and the three bases.

Double Play When two baserunners are called out on the same play.

Error A defensive mistake.

Fielder's Choice A play where the fielder puts out a baserunner rather than the batter.

Fly Ball Any ball batted into the air and caught without having touched the ground.

Foul Ball A ball batted outside of fair territory.

Foul Tip A batted ball, not higher than the batter's head, which goes right to the catcher and is caught. It counts as a strike.

Full Count Three balls and two strikes on the batter.

Grand Slam A homerun with the bases loaded.

Grounder A batted ball hit on the ground.

Home Team	The team on whose field the game is being played.
Infield	Fair territory within the base paths.
Inning	The division of a game where each team has a turn at bat and in which there are three outs for each team.
Inside Pitch	A pitched ball that misses the strike zone, on the side near the batter.
Line Drive	A batted ball that travels in a straight line.
Offensive Team	The team at bat.
On Deck	The next person to bat.
Out	The retirement of the batter or baserunner during play.
Outfield	The fair territory beyond the outfield.
Outside Pitch	A pitched ball that misses the strike zone on the side away from the batter.
Overrun	To run beyond a base.
Overthrow	To throw above the base player's or fielder's hand.
Passed Ball	A legally pitched ball that the catcher fails to hold.
Perfect Game	A game in which the pitcher allows no hits, no runs, and where no opposing player gets on base.
Pinch Hitter	A substitute batter.
Pitch Out	A pitch intentionally thrown wide so the batter will not swing at it.
Play Ball	A term used by the plate umpire to indicate that the game will begin, or play will be resumed.
Pop Up	A short, high fly in or near the infield.
RBI	Run batted in.
Sacrifice	Advancing a runner by forcing a play on the batter.
Shutout	A game in which one team fails to score.
Stealing	A baserunner trying to advance to the next base as the pitcher throws the ball to the batter.
Strike Zone	Any part of home plate between the batter's knees and armpits when using a normal batting stance.
Tag	To touch a base with ball in hand before the runner, or to touch a runner with the ball in hand.
Tag Up	On a long fly, the runner goes back to the bag and then runs after the ball is touched by a fielder.
Triple Play	Three outs that are the result of continuous action on one batted ball.
Walk	When a batter has four balls called, and may advance safely to first base.

200. SPEEDBALL FACTS

➡ The game of speedball was developed by E. D. Mitchell at the University of Michigan in the early 1920s.

➡ Mitchell developed it because of a need for a vigorous team game that could be played outdoors.

➡ Speedball is a combination of soccer, football, and basketball.

➡ It can be adapted and played indoors on a basketball court or outdoors on a soccer field.

➡ It is played on a soccer field with eleven players but can be easily modified and played indoors with fewer players.

➡ No special equipment is needed to play speedball.

201. SPEEDBALL PLAYING FIELD AND EQUIPMENT

Playing Field

➡ The game is played on a flat, level, rectangular surface, such as a soccer field or a basketball court.

➡ The game is meant to be played within the boundary lines such as the traditional lines used on a basketball court, or boundaries agreed upon by both teams prior to the start of the game.

➡ There must be goal lines, where the net must be placed and the crease is marked off; and a center circle, for the opening kickoff.

Goal Dimensions

➡ Although the size of the goal may vary, it must remain consistent for both teams.

➡ Any type of goal may be used, but soccer and football goals are the most common.

➡ The typical net size is 18 feet wide.

The Ball

➡ The ball used for all games is a semi-deflated white volleyball or soccer ball. It must have enough air in it to dribble easily.

202. BASIC RULES OF SPEEDBALL

The Game

→ Speedball is a combination of soccer, football, and basketball played by two teams of 11 players each.

→ The purpose of each team is to score into the opponent's net and to prevent the other team from securing the ball or scoring.

→ Speedball is played in quarters. Although the time for each quarter is typically 15 minutes, the game should be modified to meet the requirements of the participants.

The Play

→ The ball may be passed, thrown, tapped, rolled, dribbled, kicked, or headed in any direction.

→ In advancing the ball, the offense attempts to score either by field goal, touchdown, penalty kick, or end goal.

→ Each game starts with a kickoff at center field.

→ When continuing a game after teams switch ends, the team that gave up the last goal starts with the ball.

→ A timeout may only be called if the team asking for the timeout has possession of the ball.

→ Attacking players may be substituted for each other freely.

© 2001 Parker Publishing Company

The Goalkeeper

→ The goalkeeper may use any part of his or her body to block shots.

→ Each goalie also has a special area known as the "crease," a rectangular area directly in front of the net that no member of the opposing team may enter.

→ Players may not enter their own goalie's crease unless their team is in possession of the ball.

→ When a penalty is called, possession of the ball is given to the goaltender of the team that was not at fault for the penalty. The goalie must put the ball in play as soon as possible or face a delay-of-game penalty.

→ The goaltender may be removed from play in order to put an extra attacker on the field. This substitution may be made while the ball is in play. If a goalkeeper has been removed from play, his or her crease no longer has any effect on game play and any player may move through it freely as though it were not there.

Scoring

→ A goal is scored when the ball crosses the goal line completely between the two endposts of the goal net and below the upper crossbar.

➡ Goals are scored by either throwing (1 point), kicking (2 points), or heading (3 points) the ball into the net.

➡ The points can be adjusted to meet the needs of varying age groups or for emphasizing specific skill usage.

➡ Goals are disallowed if:

- Any player of the team that scored the goal is standing within the opposing goalie's crease when the ball crosses the goal line.

- A player who jumps as he or she throws the ball scores but then lands in the opponent's crease due to momentum.

- A player stands behind the opposing team's net and puts the ball in by reaching over the top crossbar and slamming the ball in the net.

➡ When a goal is scored, the team scored against immediately gains possession of the ball.

➡ No player from the scoring team may touch the ball until it is put into play by the goalie who was scored upon.

➡ If the game is tied, the teams will continue in a sudden death overtime for five minutes.

Types of Goals

Field Goal   Propelling the ball with the feet or body (no hands or arms) into the goal.

Touchdown   Throwing the ball across the goal line to a teammate who catches it in the end zone. A touchdown is similar to a football touchdown.

Drop Kick   Drop kicking the ball over the goal crossbar from outside the end zone. Used in scoring when using football goal posts as goals.

Penalty Kick Free kicking the ball as a result of a personal contact foul against the defending team when in its own penalty area. The ball is kicked from the penalty kick mark into the goal. It is suggested that the ball be placed on the ground similar to a soccer penalty kick rather than drop kicked.

End Goal   The offense kicking the ball over the end line from within the end zone without the ball going into the goal. It is suggested that this method of scoring not be used; instead, if the offense kicks the ball over the endline, it is suggested that the opponents receive a pass or kick-in from the spot where the ball went over the endline.

203. SPEEDBALL PENALTIES AND INFRACTIONS

Holding   Grabbing onto a player with both hands in an attempt to obstruct his or her forward motion or prevent him or her from throwing the ball.

Tripping   Tripping a player to jar the ball loose or slow him or her down.

Interference   Making contact with the goaltender to move him or her out of position or to steal the ball from the goaltender.

Charging   Running at a fast speed into an opposing player.

Roughing   Overly excessive contact with another player.

Intent to Injure   An attempt to injure a player in order to remove him or her from the game.

Fighting   Engaging in a fight with another player.

Instigation   Deliberately baiting a player into a fight.

Too Many Players on the Field

Delay of Game

Penalties Are Assessed as Follows:

➡ Minor penalties, 2 minutes.

➡ Major penalties (usually with an excessive amount of violence and/or an injury being the result), 5 minutes.

➡ Misconduct (usually the result of an excessive major penalty) results in ejection from the game.

➡ Penalties are only assessed once a player from the team that violated the rule has possession of the ball.

Infractions

➡ A defensive player going through the crease without possession of the ball results in a penalty shot.

➡ When offside or a disallowed goal is called, the opposing team's goalie gets the ball once play restarts.

Penalty Shots

➡ All players except the one awarded the shot and the opposing goaltender are required to leave the field.

➡ The remaining player is given the ball just inside the offensive zone.

➡ He or she gets one shot on the goalkeeper.

➡ If the player scores, his or her team is awarded one point, and play resumes, with the defending goalkeeper gaining control of the ball.

➡ If the shot is missed or blocked, the defending goalkeeper gets possession of the ball.

204. SPEEDBALL TERMS

Aerial Ball The legal conversion of a ground ball using the feet to lift or kick it into the hands. When it is in the hands, it can be thrown, passed, and caught as in football and basketball. The ball can be air dribbled to oneself only one time each possession. The air dribble consists of throwing the ball in the air and catching it to regain possession. On the air dribble, steps do not count while the ball is in the air. A player is legally allowed one step with the ball when holding it if obtained while standing, or two steps if running prior to receiving it. Additional steps are illegal and are called traveling. Holding the ball with the hands for more than three seconds without giving up possession is illegal. This speeds up the game and is a rule that can be modified.

Free Kick Certain identified infractions result in a free kick which is identical to soccer except that the opponents only need to be five yards from the ball. The kick is taken at the spot of the infraction. An indirect free kick means that someone must touch the ball before a goal can be scored.

Ground Ball When the ball is on the ground (rolling, bouncing, or stationary), it is played as it is in soccer with skills of dribbling, kicking, heading, or trapping. In order for the ball to be thrown, it must first be brought from the feet immediately into the hands.

Jump Ball (Toss Up, Tie Ball) Two opponents simultaneously holding the ball results in a jump ball. If it is not possible to decide which team put the ball out-of-bounds, a jump ball is held. The format is the same as in basketball with two opponents facing each other and jumping to tip the ball which is tossed between them. All other opponents must be at least five yards away. The ball remains as an aerial ball off the tip provided it does not contact the ground, in which case it is considered a ground ball.

Out-of-Bounds   A ball going off the field of play over the sideline is put back in play with a throw-in as in basketball. A ball over the endline is either thrown or kicked into play.

Penalty Kick   Certain foul situations result in this free kick. The ball is placed on the penalty kick line, and one of the offended team members is allowed a free kick to attempt to score a field goal against the opposing team goalie. The offensive team members are positioned outside the defender's penalty area. The defensive players, aside from the goalie, are positioned either behind the endline or outside the penalty area.

Physical Contact   Rules allow for the same body contact as in soccer when the ball is on the ground. With the ball in the hands, guarding as in basketball is appropriate.

217. HISTORICAL FACTS ABOUT TRACK AND FIELD

➡ The marathon can be traced to the Ancient Olympic Games in Greece in 776 B.C.

➡ Babe Didrikson, believed to be the greatest female athlete of her era, overwhelmed her opponents in three Olympic Track and Field events in 1932.

➡ Jesse Owens won four Olympic gold medals in Track and Field in 1936.

➡ Abebe Bikila, an Ethiopian, won the marathon running barefoot in the 1960 Rome Olympics, and again in 1964 in Tokyo, this time running in shoes.

➡ Wilma Rudolph overcame childhood diseases to win three Olympic gold medals in 1960.

➡ Wyomia Tyus was named the fastest woman in the world in 1964 and again in Mexico in 1968.

➡ Ten world records were set in 1968 and 26 out of a possible 30 Olympic records were shattered.

➡ Dick Fosbury, creator of the "Fosbury flop," revolutionized the high jump event.

➡ Bob Beamon redefined the long jump when he shattered the previous record with a remarkable leap of 29 feet 2 $^1/_2$ inches.

➡ Carl Lewis mirrored the accomplishment of his idol, Jesse Owens, by winning four gold medals in the 1984 Olympic Games in Los Angeles.

218. TRACK AND FIELD EQUIPMENT

Besides running shoes used by (nearly) all competitors, equipment needs for Track and Field events come almost exclusively from the Field category.

Discus Throw

- The men's discus weighs 2 kilograms (4 pounds 6 1/2 ounces).
- The women's discus weighs 1 kilogram (2 pounds 3 1/4 ounces).

Hammer Throw

- A 16-pound metal sphere attached to a grip by means of a spring steel wire not longer than 3 feet 11 3/4 inches.

High Jump

- The crossbar is 4 meters long and the runway must be at least 20 meters long.

Javelin

- The men's javelin must weigh a minimum of 800 grams (1 pound 12 1/4 ounces) and measure between 2.6 meters and 2.7 meters.
- The women's javelin must weigh a minimum of 600 grams (26.16 ounces) and measure between 2.2 meters and 2.3 meters.

- The shaft of the javelin may be either wood or metal.

Pole Vault

- The pole may be of any length and made of any material or combination of materials.
- The runway must be at least 40 meters long, preferably at least 45 meters.

- The crossbar is 4.5 meters long.

Shot Put

- A shot is a ball made of iron or brass.
- Men use a 16-pound shot.
- Women use a shot that weighs 8 pounds 14 3/4 ounces.

219. TRACK AND FIELD DIAGRAMS

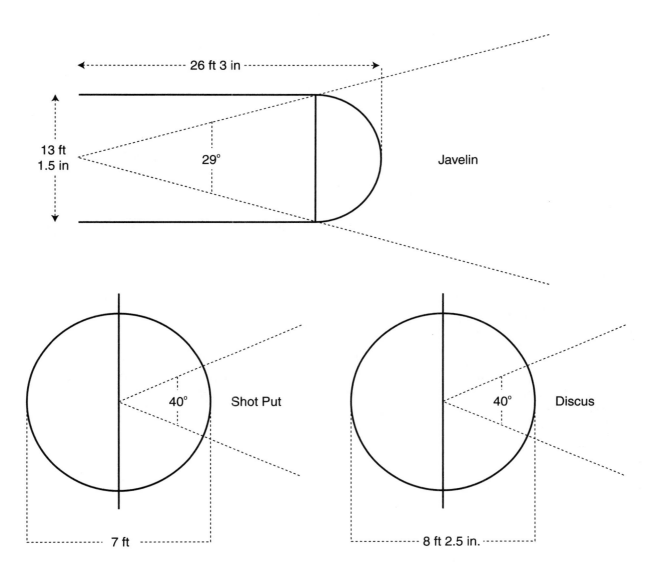

220. BASIC RULES OF TRACK AND FIELD

➡ Track and Field requires far-ranging and incredibly diverse physical skills.

➡ All races are started by the firing of a gun by an official at the starting line.

➡ For races up to and including one lap of an outdoor track, the runners must stay for the entire distance within lanes marked on the track.

➡ There may be six to eight lanes, with each lane usually measuring 1.2 meter (4 feet) in width.

➡ The winner in each race is the runner whose *torso* first passes the finish line.

➡ Races are timed either by mechanical watches or by more sophisticated, electronic photo-timers that can measure finishes to the hundredth of a second.

➡ Qualifying rounds, or heats, are sometimes held to narrow down the contestants to the fastest runners.

➡ Athletes in the field events may also have qualifying rounds.

➡ In the horizontal jumps and throws, athletes are allowed three preliminary attempts if the field numbers more than eight participants. The best performers are then given three more attempts.

➡ In the vertical jumps, the high jump, and the pole vault, the participants are permitted to continue until they have three successive failures. If two or more contestants tie, the competitor with the fewest failures at the last height cleared is the winner. If still tied, the total number of failures is the deciding factor.

➡ Scoring systems may differ according to the meet.

221. TRACK EVENTS

Sprints

➠ Sprinting is short-distance running in which the runner tries to maintain full speed for the whole race.

➠ The 100-meter and the 200-meter are the two main sprint races.

➠ Sprints:

- 100-meter
- 200-meter
- 400-meter

Relays

➠ A relay race is made up of four sprints of equal distance put together.

➠ Each equal distance is called a leg that is run by one of four teammates, the last of whom is called the anchor.

➠ Medley relays are races where the legs are of different distances.

➠ The most popular relays are the 4 × 100 meter (which means each of the four runners runs a 100-meter dash) and the 4 × 400 meter.

➠ The relay runner must carry a foot-long baton that he or she needs to pass smoothly and quickly to the next runner in the relay.

➠ Relays:

- 4 × 100-meter relay
- 4 × 200-meter relay
- 4 × 400-meter relay
- 4 × 800-meter relay
- 4 × 1500-meter relay
- 4 × 1 mile relay

Hurdling

➠ Hurdling is sprinting while having to clear hurdles of up to 42 inches.

➠ High hurdles are 42 inches high, intermediate hurdles are 36 inches high, and low hurdles are 30 inches high.

➠ Hurdles:

- 110-meter (men)
- 100-meter (women)
- 400-meter

Middle-Distance Running

➡ Middle-distance races include all races over 400 meters through the mile.

➡ The two most popular middle-distance races are the 800-meter run and the mile run.

➡ Middle distances:

- 800-meter
- 1000-meter (indoors only)
- 1500-meter (the "metric mile")
- 1 mile

Long-Distance Running (Cross-Country)

➡ Races longer than 3,000 meters are considered long-distance events.

➡ Cross-country races are run over rough terrain while other distance races are held on flat tracks of varying composition.

➡ No world records are kept for cross-country racing due to the varying conditions and sites.

➡ Cross-country races seldom exceed 14.5 kilometers (9 miles).

➡ The marathon, which is normally run on a paved road, is run over a course of 42 kilometers 194 meters (26 miles 385 yards).

➡ The steeplechase is an obstacle race, usually run over a 3,000-meter course containing hurdles, water jumps, and other hazards.

➡ Long distances:

- 3000-meter
- 5000-meter
- 10,000-meter
- Marathon
- Steeplechase

222. FIELD EVENTS

High Jump

→ The goal in high jumping is to leap over and clear a crossbar that rests at increasing heights between two upright standards about 4 meters (13 feet) apart.

→ The high jumper is permitted three attempts to clear each height.

→ Most jumpers use the style known as the "Fosbury flop."

→ The Fosbury flop was named for its originator, American jumper Dick Fosbury, who used the style to win the high jump in the 1968 Olympics.

→ To execute the Fosbury flop, jumpers approach the crossbar straight on, leap and twist on takeoff, rise above the bar headfirst, clear the bar with their backs toward the ground, and land on the mat with their shoulders.

→ In the high jump, heights are measured perpendicularly from the ground to the lowest point of the crossbar.

→ Jumpers may not:

- Take off from both feet.
- Dislodge the bar from its pegs.
- Touch the landing area beyond the plane of the uprights without clearing the bar.

→ If there is a tie:

- The competitor with the least amount of jumps at the height wins.
- If the tie still remains, the person with the lowest amount of failures at the end of the competition wins.
- If the tie still remains, the person with the least amount of total jumps taken is the winner.
- Four different types of jumps are the *scissors*, the *western roll*, the *straddle*, and the *Fosbury flop*.

Pole Vault

→ In pole vaulting, the athlete attempts to clear a high crossbar using a 4- to 5-meter (12- to 16-foot) long flexible pole.

→ The pole is typically made of fiberglass.

→ Grasping the pole several feet from its top, the vaulter races down a short runway, digs the tip of the pole into a box or slot in the ground, and swings upward toward the crossbar.

→ As the jumper's feet near the bar, he or she thrusts his or her body face down over and across the bar.

→ The vaulter then drops onto a soft pad called the pit.

→ Jumpers are permitted three attempts at each height.

➥ The height is typically increased by 8 to 15 centimeters (3 to 6 inches) at a time.

➥ Three misses at a given height disqualifies a vaulter and the competitor is given credit for the greatest height cleared.

➥ Misses are charged when an athlete dislodges the bar, passes to the side of or underneath the bar, touches the ground beyond with the pole, switches hands, or moves the upper hand on the pole after leaving the ground.

➥ Vaults are measured perpendicularly from the upper side of the bar to the ground.

Long Jump (Broad Jump)

➥ The contestant runs along a runway and springs into the air from a point called the takeoff board.

➥ The length of the run varies from person to person.

➥ Fouling occurs if the jumper steps over the board or runs past the plane of the board, even if he or she makes no attempt to jump.

➥ His or her goal is to travel the greatest possible distance before landing.

➥ The jumper throws both feet far forward while still in the air to increase the distance and to prepare to land.

➥ The best seven performers after three jumps take three additional jumps.

➥ A jump is measured along a straight line extending from the front edge of the takeoff board to the landing mark made closest to the takeoff board by *any part* of the jumper's body.

Triple Jump

➥ The triple jump consists of three distinct sections:
  • Hop—Athlete takes off and lands on the same foot as that from which he or she had taken off.
  • Step—Athlete lands on the other foot from that used for the hop.
  • Jump—Athlete jumps from one foot and lands on one or both feet in the sand pit.

➥ A foul jump is recorded if:
  • Any part of the athlete's takeoff foot extends over the front line or side edge of the takeoff mat or board.
  • The athlete walks back through the pit after the jump.
  • In the course of landing, the athlete touches the ground outside the landing area.

➥ The run-up may not exceed 40 meters.

➥ The athlete must land in the pit in order for the jump to be valid.

© 2001 Parker Publishing Company

Shot Put

→ The aim in shot putting is to propel a solid metal ball through the air for maximum distance.

→ The men's shot weighs 7.26 kilograms (16 pounds).

→ The women's shot weighs 4 kilograms (8 pounds 14 $3/4$ ounces).

→ The participant is confined to a 2.1-meter (7-foot) circle.

→ The put must be made from the shoulder with one arm only, and the shot may not be brought behind the shoulder.

→ The shot must land within a clearly marked sector for the throw to be valid.

Discus

→ The discus is a heavy disc thrown from inside a circle to a wedge-shaped marked area of the field.

→ The discus is made of wood with a metal rim and weighted interior.

→ The men's discus is 8.7 inches in diameter and weighs 2 kilograms (4 pounds $6 1/2$ ounces).

→ The women's is 7.1 inches in diameter and weighs 1 kilogram (2 pounds $3 1/4$ ounces).

→ The circle is 2.5 meters (8 feet $2 1/2$ inches) in diameter, and has a nonslip surface that is banded by a metal ring.

→ The sector lines are two white lines extending out from the circle at a 40-degree angle.

→ The participant must begin from a stationary position with his or her back to a marked sector.

→ The participant must stay within the circle until the discus has landed and the discus must land between the sector lines.

→ Throws are measured from the nearest mark made by the discus to the inner edge of the circle's ring.

→ Three qualifying throws are taken, and then the finalists make three final throws.

Hammer Throw

➡ Hammer throwers compete by hurling a heavy ball that is attached to a length of wire and a metal handle.

➡ The ball, wire, and handle together weigh 7.26 kilograms (16 pounds) and form a unit no longer than 1.2 meters (4 feet).

➡ The athlete is confined to a circle 2.1 meters (7 feet) in diameter.

➡ While gripping the handle with both hands and keeping the feet stationary, the athlete whirls the ball around in a circle passing above and behind the head and just below the kneecaps.

➡ The hammer is then released upward and outward at a 45-degree angle.

➡ Each thrower gets three tries, after which the seven best performers are permitted three more tries.

➡ A foul (violation) is called when any part of the competitor's body, or the hammer itself, touches the ground in or outside the circle before the hammer has been fairly released and has struck the ground.

➡ A 15.9-kilogram (35-pound) weight is used in indoor meets.

Javelin

➡ The javelin is a steel-tipped metal spear, with a minimum length of 260 centimeters (8 feet 6.25 inches) for men and 220 centimeters (7 feet 2.5 inches) for women.

➡ The javelin has a minimum weight of 800 grams (1.75 pounds) for men and 600 grams (1.5 pounds) for women.

➡ The javelin has a grip made of whipcord about 15 centimeters (approximately 6 inches) long, which is located at the center of gravity.

➡ Two parallel lines, 4 meters (13 feet 1.5 inches) apart, mark the javelin runway.

➡ The throwing line is a 7-centimeter (2.75-inch) wide strip, which touches the front ends of the runway lines.

➡ The center of this strip is an equal distance from and located between the runway lines.

➡ From this center point two straight lines extend through the ends of the scratch line for a distance of 90 meters (29.5 feet).

➡ All throws must land tip first between these lines. Throws are measured on a direct line from point of impact to the center point.

➡ Throwers must stay within the runway and may not touch or cross the throwing line.

➡ The contestants hold the javelin near its center of gravity and run towards the throw line.

➡ Contestants get three throws, and the seven best throwers are given three additional throws.

Decathlon/Heptathlon

➡ The men's decathlon is a 2-day, 10-event contest that includes, in order, the 100-meter dash, long jump, shot put, high jump, 400-meter run, 110-meter high hurdles, discus throw, pole vault, javelin throw, and 1500-meter run.

➡ The athlete's performance in the various events is rated against an ideal score of 10,000 points.

➡ The women's heptathlon is a 2-day, 7-event contest that includes the 100-meter hurdles, shot put, high jump, long jump, 200-meter run, 800-meter run, and javelin throw.

Pentathlon

➡ The pentathlon includes pistol shooting, fencing, swimming, an equestrian event, and cross-country running.

➡ Contestants fire shots at rotating targets in the pistol-shooting event.

➡ The fencing portion is a round-robin tournament with a single touch deciding each match.

➡ The swimming course is 300 meters (328 yards) for men and 200 meters (219 yards) for women.

➡ The equestrian event is a 600-meter (656-yard) stadium jumping event.

➡ The cross-country running course is 4000 meters (2.5 miles) for men and 2000 meters (1.24 miles) for women.

➡ Points are awarded for each individual performance, and the contestant with the highest point total after the five events is declared the winner.

Walking

➡ Walking events are usually held for distances ranging from 1500 to 50,000 meters (0.9 to 31 miles).

➡ In race walking, the heel of the forward foot must touch the track before the toe of the trailing foot leaves the ground in order to prevent the contestants from running.

223. HISTORICAL FACTS ABOUT VOLLEYBALL

➡ Volleyball was developed in 1895 by William G. Morgan at the Young Men's Christian Association (YMCA) in Holyoke, Massachusetts.

➡ It was created for businessmen who required a game that involved less physical contact than basketball.

➡ Volleyball blended elements of baseball, basketball, handball, and tennis.

➡ Volleyball was originally played using a tennis net hung 6 feet 6 inches above the floor.

➡ The first game of volleyball was played on July 7, 1896 at Springfield College.

➡ Official volleyball was designed in 1900.

➡ The set and spike were introduced in the Philippines in 1916.

➡ The United States Volleyball Association (USVBA, now called USA Volleyball) was formed in 1928.

➡ Volleyball was introduced to the Olympic Games in Tokyo in 1964.

➡ The Association of Volleyball Professionals (AVP) was formed in 1983.

➡ U.S. men's team won the Gold medal and the U.S. women's team won the Silver medal at the 1984 Olympics in Los Angeles.

➡ U.S. men's team won the Gold medal at the 1988 Olympics in Korea.

➡ Volleyball celebrated 100 years of existence in 1995.

➡ Two-person beach volleyball was added to the Olympics in 1996.

224. VOLLEYBALL PLAYER ROTATION

➡ Players rotate in a clockwise position.

➡ Position of players in order of the serve:

- Right Back
- Right Front
- Center Front
- Left Front
- Left Back
- Center Back

➡ Position of players at net:

| LF | CF | RF |
| LB | CB | RB |

225. VOLLEYBALL EQUIPMENT

The Net

➡ The net is placed vertically over the center line.

➡ The top of the net is set at the height of 2.43 meters (7 feet 11⅝ inches) for men and 2.24 meters (7 feet 4¼ inches) for women.

➡ Its height is measured from the center of the playing court.

➡ The net is 1 meter wide and 9.50 meters long, and is made of square black mesh.

The Ball

➡ The ball is spherical, and is made of a flexible leather or synthetic leather with a bladder inside made of rubber or a similar material.

➡ It may be a uniform light color or combination of colors.

➡ The volleyball measures 65 to 67 centimeters (25 to 27 inches) in circumference and weighs 260 to 280 grams.

226. VOLLEYBALL COURT

The size of the volleyball court will depend on the playing ability level and the equipment used. Dimensions will range from approximately 20 feet wide by 40 feet long for lawn or backyard volleyball to 19 feet 6 inches wide by 59 feet long for tournament play. The width of the court is determined by the size of the net used. The service areas should be a minimum of 6 feet in depth back of the endlines.

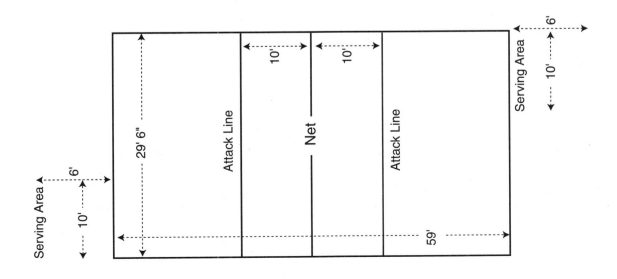

227. BASIC RULES OF VOLLEYBALL

General Rules

➡ Volleyball is played by two teams of six players on a court divided by a net.

➡ There are different versions available for specific circumstances in order to offer the versatility of the game to everyone.

➡ The object of the game is to send the ball over the net so that the opposing team cannot return the ball or prevent it from hitting the ground in their court.

➡ Each team has three hits to attempt to return the ball.

➡ The ball is put in play with a serve that is hit by the server over the net to the opponents.

➡ The volley continues until the ball hits the playing court, goes out of bounds, or a team fails to return it properly.

➡ When the receiving team wins a volley, it gains the right to serve, and the players rotate one position clockwise.

➡ When the serving team wins a volley, it wins a point and the right to continue serving.

➡ Each team consists of no more than six persons, with each side having an equal number.

➡ Each player must be in his or her own position before the ball is served.

➡ After the server strikes the ball, each player may cover any section of the court.

➡ The positions of the players are numbered as follows:

- The three players along the net are front-row players and occupy positions 4 (front left), 3 (front center), and 2 (front right).

- The other three are back-row players occupying positions 5 (back left), 6 (back center), and 1 (back right).

➡ Each player serves in turn and continues to serve until the volley is lost (side out).

➡ The ball must clear the net on the serve, unless the ball hits the net and goes over the net on the first attempt, then it may be reserved.

➡ After a team has lost its serve, the team receiving the ball for the first serve must rotate one position clockwise before serving.

➡ The ball may be volleyed only three times from one team member to another before returning it over the net.

➡ During this volley a player may not hit the ball twice in succession. One or both hands may be used.

Fouls

➡ A player holds or throws the ball.

➡ The ball touches any part of the body, other than the hands or forearms.

➡ A player touches the net with any part of the body or hands, or reaches over the net.

➡ A player plays out of position when the ball is being served.

Errors

➡ A player does not clearly hit the ball or allows the ball to come to rest on any part or parts of the body.

➡ A player hits the ball out of the boundaries of the court.

➡ A player allows the ball to hit the floor, or any object outside or over the court (except net), before being legally returned to the opponent's court.

➡ A player touches the ball twice in succession.

➡ A player fails to make a good serve.

Penalty

➡ The penalty for fouls or errors committed is a *point* if the foul or error was committed against the serving team, or *side out* if the foul or error was committed against the receiving team.

Scoring

➡ Only the serving team can score.

➡ When the serving team fails to score, it is *side out* and the receiving team becomes the serving team.

➡ The game is played to 21 points or, upon agreement by both teams, 15 points may constitute a game.

➡ A match consists of two out of three games.

228. SAFETY HINTS FOR VOLLEYBALL

➡ Warm up thoroughly prior to game.

➡ Equipment should be checked for safety prior to game.

➡ Area surrounding court or playing area must be kept free of obstacles.

➡ No jewelry or sharp objects should be worn during game.

➡ Players should stay in control and maintain their own positions.

➡ Ball should be rolled to opponents when returning ball for serve.

➡ Players should learn to play the ball properly to avoid injuries to hands and fingers.

229. VOLLEYBALL TERMS

Ace Serve that results directly in a point.

Add Out Team that has scored a point following a tie at scores over 14 points.

Block Defensive play by one or more players used to intercept a spiked ball in an attempt to rebound it back into the opponent's court.

Bump Forearm pass.

Deuce Any tie score of 14 points or more.

Dig Passing a spiked or powerfully hit ball.

Foul Violation of the rules.

Game Point Last point in a game.

Newcomb Game variation using catching and throwing skills in place of setting and bumping.

Out of Bounds When a ball lands completely outside of the boundary lines.

Pancake Defensive technique where player extends hand, palm down on floor, so that ball bounces off back of hand.

Rotation Clockwise movement of players prior to the new serving term of a team.

Serve Skill used by player in back-right position to put ball into play.

Side Out When serving team fails to win the point or makes an illegal play.

230. WEIGHT TRAINING FACTS

➡ Weight training trains and develops the muscles for power, the ability of the muscle to do maximum work within the shortest amount of time.

➡ Strength training increases bone density and tendon and ligament thickness, and decreases the risk of injury by increasing overall structural strength.

➡ Muscle atrophies at a rate of about 6.6 pounds per decade of age past 20 years old if not exercised.

➡ Strength training can avoid muscle atrophy due to the aging process.

231. BENEFITS OF WEIGHT TRAINING

➡ Helps control blood pressure

➡ Reduces body fat

➡ Improves posture

➡ Increases muscle strength

➡ Raises basal metabolic rate

➡ Increases bone density

➡ Prevents injury from normal activities

➡ Improves physical appearance

232. GUIDELINES TO FOLLOW WHEN LIFTING WEIGHTS

➡ Lift weights from the floor with legs and not the back.

➡ Use a smooth full range of motion.

➡ Don't jerk the weights.

➡ Don't lock the knees (keep them slightly bent).

➡ Don't put pressure on the teeth because the enamel can crack.

➡ Don't flex or hyperextend the back.

➡ Always concentrate during lifting.

➡ Unoxygenated muscles can cramp; breathe on exertion.

➡ Always stretch prior to lifting, work up to maximum desired weight, and then work back down to starting weight.

Free-Weights Spotters

➡ It is important to use a spotter whenever free weights are raised over the lifter's head.

➡ A spotter's responsibility is to insure the safety of the user during the execution of the exercise.

➡ The spotter must observe the condition of the user and try to anticipate exhaustion.

➡ The spotter must also insure that balance and an even lift are executed, that proper breathing technique is adhered to, and that proper form is being executed by the user.

Determining the Amount of Weight to Be Lifted

➡ A repetition is referred to as a *rep* and is a single lift of the weights.

➡ A group of reps is called a *set*.

➡ An exercise is generally composed of 3 to 4 sets.

➡ The amount of weights to use is dependent on the goal and fitness level of the participant.

➡ If the goal is to build muscle at the fastest rate, then 6 to 8 repetitions should be done with a heavier weight.

➡ If the goal is building or toning, then 8 to 12 repetitions should be done with a medium weight.

➡ If the goal is to simply tone or maintain the existing muscle strength, then 12 to 16 repetitions should be done with a lighter weight.

➡ Participants should never use the heavy weight category if they have not lifted before or if significant amount of time has passed since they have last trained.

➡ When initially beginning a training program, it is recommended to use the lighter weights for at least 3 to 4 weeks before progressing to the medium weights.

➡ A basic method that can be used to determine the weight to use for a particular exercise is to simply estimate the initial weight.

➡ A participant should complete as many as possible.

➡ If the goal is to build muscle at the fastest rate and the participant can complete more than 8 reps, the weight is too light. If the participant cannot complete more than 6 reps, then the weight is too heavy.

➡ According to the American College of Sport Medicine (ACSM), the recommended minimum weight training is one set of 8 to 12 repetitions of eight to ten exercises that work the major muscle groups at least two times per week.

233. ORDER OF MUSCLE GROUPS WHEN EXERCISING

Prior to strength training, warm-up and flexibility exercises should be performed. The warm-up should include at least 5 minutes of aerobic activity to provide increased blood oxygen levels and increased body temperature, which will increase the effectiveness of the strength-training workout.

Exercise sessions should be organized so that the larger muscle groups are exercised first, followed by the smaller muscle groups. For example:

➡ Abdomen

➡ Hips and lower back

➡ Upper legs

➡ Calves

➡ Chest

➡ Upper back

➡ Shoulders

➡ Triceps

➡ Biceps

➡ Waist

➡ Neck

234. MUSCLES EXERCISED BY SPECIFIC EXERCISES

1. **Chest Exercises**	**Muscle Groups**
Bench Press	Pectorals, Triceps, Deltoids
Inclined Fly	Pectorals, Anterior Deltoids
Inclined Press	Upper, Pectorals, Triceps, Deltoids
Declined Press	Pectorals, Triceps, Deltoids
Push-up	Triceps, Anterior Deltoids

2. **Back Exercises**	**Muscle Groups**
Shrugs	Trapezius
One-Arm Row	Trapezius, Latissimus Dorsi
Pull-up	Biceps, Rhomboids
Back Extension	Erector Spinae
Seated Row	Erector Spinae, Latissimus Dorsi, Biceps
Lateral Pull-Down	Latissimus Dorsi, Biceps

3. **Shoulder Exercises**   **Muscle Groups**

   Overhead (Military) Press   Deltoid, Triceps

   Lateral Raises   Deltoid

   Front Raises   Deltoid

   Prone Fly   Deltoid, Rhomboids

4. **Arm Exercises**   **Muscle Groups**

   Barbell Curl   Biceps, Forearms

   Dumbbell Preacher Curl   Biceps

   Seated Hammer Curls   Biceps, Forearms (Brachialis)

   Seated Inclined Curls   Biceps

   Seated Overhead Extension   Triceps

   Lying Extension   Triceps

5. **Lower Body Exercises**   **Muscle Groups**

   Squat   Gluteus Maximus, Quads, Hamstrings

   Front Lunge   Gluteus Maximus, Quads, Hamstrings

   Calf Heel Raise   Gastrocnemius, Soleus

   Hip Extension   Gluteus Maximus

   Hip Abduction   Abductors, Outer Thigh

   Hip Adduction   Adductor, Inner Thigh

   Leg Press   Gluteus Maximus, Quads, Hamstrings

   Leg Extension   Quads

   Leg Curl   Hamstrings

6. **Abdominal Exercises**   **Muscle Groups**

   Crunches/Inclined Sit-up   Upper Abdomen

   Crunches/Leg Raises   Lower Abdomen

   Side Crunches   Outer Obliques

Guides

240. TABLE OF WEIGHTS AND MEASURES

➡ METRIC SYSTEM

Length

1 millimeter	=	1/1000 meter
1 centimeter	=	1/100 meter
1 decimeter	=	1/10 meter
1 meter	=	10 decimeters
1 meter	=	100 centimeters
1 kilometer	=	1000 meters

Weight

1 gram	=	1000 milligrams
1 kilogram	=	1000 grams

➡ UNITED STATES

Length

1 foot	=	12 inches
1 yard	=	3 feet
1 yard	=	36 inches
1 mile	=	1760 yards
1 mile	=	5280 feet

Weight

1 pound	=	16 ounces

241. METRIC CONVERSION TABLE

	TO CONVERT	TO	MULTIPLY BY
Length	centimeters	inches	0.394
	meters	feet	3.281
	meters	yards	1.0936
	kilometers	miles	0.62
	inches	centimeters	2.54
	feet	meters	0.3048
	yards	meters	0.914
	miles	kilometers	1.609
Weight	grams	ounces	0.0353
	kilograms	pounds	2.2046
	ounces	grams	28.35
	pounds	kilograms	0.4536

1 KILOMETER = 1000 METERS

242. METRIC AND U.S. EQUIVALENTS

➡ 1 meter = 39.37 inches = 3.2808 feet = 1.0936 yards

➡ 1 kilometer = 1000 meters = 0.621370 mile

➡ 5 k = 3.1 miles

➡ 10 k = 6.2 miles

➡ 20 k = 12.4 miles

➡ 30 k = 18.6 miles

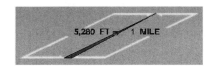
5,280 FT = 1 MILE

FEET		METERS	FEET		METERS
1	=	0.305	20	=	6.096
2	=	0.610	30	=	9.144
3	=	0.914	40	=	12.192
4	=	1.219	50	=	15.240
5	=	1.524	60	=	18.288
6	=	1.829	70	=	21.336
7	=	2.134	80	=	24.384
8	=	2.438	90	=	27.432
9	=	2.743	100	=	30.480
10	=	3.048	200	=	60.690

YARDS		METERS	MILES		METERS
40	=	36.56	1	=	1609.3
50	=	45.70	2	=	3218.7
60	=	54.84	3	=	4828.0
70	=	63.98	4	=	6437.4
75	=	68.55	5	=	8046.7
100	=	91.40	6	=	9656.1
110	=	100.54	7	=	11265.4
120	=	109.68	8	=	12874.8
220	=	201.08	9	=	14484.1
300	=	274.20	10	=	16093.5
440	=	402.16			
600	=	548.40			
880	=	804.32			
1000	=	914.00			
1320	=	1206.48			

1 INCH

1 YARD IS EQUAL TO 36 INCHES

243. INTERESTING OLYMPIC FACTS

The Olympic Flag

➡ Created by Baron Pierre de Coubertin in 1914, the Olympic flag contains five interconnected rings on a white background.

➡ The five rings symbolize five geographic areas—Europe, Asia, Africa, Australia, and the U.S.—and are interconnected to symbolize the friendship to be gained from these international competitions.

➡ The rings, from left to right, are blue, yellow, black, green, and red.

➡ The colors were chosen because at least one of them has appeared on the flag of every country in the world.

➡ The Olympic flag was first flown during the 1920 Olympic Games.

The Olympic Motto

➡ In 1921, Baron de Coubertin borrowed a Latin phrase from his friend, Father Henri Didon, for the Olympic motto: "Citius, Altius, Fortius" ("Swifter, Higher, Stronger").

The Olympic Oath

➡ Baron de Coubertin wrote the oath for the athletes to recite at each of the Olympic Games.

➡ During the opening ceremonies, one athlete recites the oath on behalf of all the athletes.

➡ The Olympic oath was first taken by Belgian fencer Victor Boin.

➡ The Olympic Oath states, "In the name of all competitors I promise that we shall take part in these Olympic Games, respecting and abiding by the rules that govern them, in the true spirit of sportsmanship for the glory of sport and the honor of our teams."

The Olympic Creed

➡ Baron de Coubertin got the idea for the creed from a speech given by Bishop Ethelbert Talbot at a service for Olympic champions during the 1908 Olympic Games.

➡ The words of the creed have been displayed on the scoreboard at every modern Olympic Games since 1908.

➡ The Olympic Creed reads, "The most important thing in the Olympic Games is not to win but to take part, just as the most important thing in life is not the triumph but the struggle. The essential thing is not to have conquered but to have fought well."

The Olympic Flame

➡ The Olympic flame is a practice continued from the ancient Olympic Games.

➡ In Olympia (Greece), a flame was ignited by the sun and then kept burning until the closing of the Olympic Games.

➡ The flame first appeared in the modern Olympics at the 1928 Olympic Games in Amsterdam.

➡ The flame itself represents a number of things, including purity and the endeavor for perfection.

➡ The chairman of the organizing committee for the 1936 Olympic Games, Carl Diem, suggested what is now the modern Olympic Torch relay.

➡ Women wearing ancient-style robes and using a curved mirror and the sun light the Olympic flame at the ancient site of Olympia.

➡ The Olympic Torch is then passed from runner to runner from the ancient site of Olympia to the Olympic stadium in the hosting city. (Ships and planes are used when necessary.)

➡ The flame is then kept alight until the Games have concluded.

➡ The Olympic Torch relay represents a continuation from the ancient Olympic Games to the modern Olympics.

The Olympic Hymn

➡ The Olympic Hymn, played when the Olympic Flag is raised, was composed by Spyros Samaras and the words added by Kostis Palamas.

➡ The Olympic Hymn was first played at the 1896 Olympic Games in Athens, but wasn't declared the official hymn by the IOC until 1957.

The Olympic Medals

➡ The last Olympic gold medals that were made entirely out of gold were awarded in 1912.

➡ The Olympic medals are designed especially for each individual Olympic Games by the host city's organizing committee.

➡ Each medal must be at least 3 millimeters thick and 60 millimeters in diameter.

➡ The gold and silver Olympic medals must be made out of 92.5 percent silver, with the gold medal covered in six grams of gold.

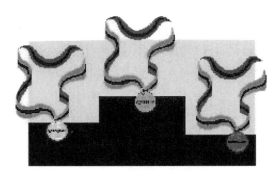

© 2001 Parker Publishing Company

The Exact Length of a Marathon

➡ During the first several modern Olympics, the marathon was always an approximate distance.

➡ The British royal family in 1908 requested that the marathon start at Windsor Castle so that the royal children could witness the start.

➡ The distance from Windsor Castle to the Olympic Stadium was 42,195 meters (or 26 miles 385 yards).

➡ This distance became the standardized length of a marathon in 1924.

Stadium

➡ The first recorded ancient Olympic Games were held in 776 B.C. with only one event—the *stade*.

➡ The stade was a unit of measurement (about 600 feet) that also became the name of the race because it was the distance run.

➡ Since the track for the stade was a stade in length, the location of the race became the *stadium*.

Gymnasium

➡ The word "gymnasium" comes from the Greek root *gymnos* meaning nude.

➡ The literal meaning of "gymnasium" is "school for naked exercise."

➡ Athletes in the ancient Olympic Games participated in the nude.

Counting Olympiads

➡ An Olympiad is a period of four successive years.

➡ The Olympic Games celebrate each Olympiad.

➡ For the modern Olympic Games, the first Olympiad celebration was in 1896.

➡ Every four years celebrates another Olympiad; therefore, even the Games that were canceled count as Olympiads.

Interesting Olympic Facts

➡ The first opening ceremonies were held during the 1908 Olympic Games in London.

➡ During the opening ceremony of the Olympic Games, the procession of athletes is always led by the Greek team, followed by all the other teams in alphabetical order (in the language of the hosting country), except for the last team, which is always the team of the hosting country.

➡ When choosing locations for the Olympic Games, the IOC specifically gives the honor of holding the Games to a city rather than a country.

244. THE GAMES OF THE OLYMPIADS AND THE CITIES OF THE OLYMPIC GAMES

An Olympiad is a period of four years, the beginning of which is marked by the celebration of the Olympic Games. Each Olympiad is designated by Roman numerals. The year in which the Olympic Games are to be held cannot be changed. If the Games are canceled for any reason, the number of the Olympiad remains. Only the "Summer" Games are Games of the Olympiad. The term "Olympiad" does not apply to the Olympic Winter Games. The term "Olympic" actually is an adjective, not a noun. Properly speaking, an athlete competes in the Olympic Games, not the Olympics. The phrases "Summer and Winter Olympics" are commonly used, but they are technically incorrect references to the Games of the Olympiad and the Olympic Winter Games.

The following is a list of the Olympiads of the modern era with the Games of the Olympiads and a list of the Olympic Winter Games.

Games of the Olympiad

I	1896	Athens, Greece
II	1900	Paris, France
III	1904	St. Louis, U.S.A.
IV	1908	London, England
V	1912	Stockholm, Sweden
VI	1916	Canceled due to WWI
VII	1920	Antwerp, Belgium
VIII	1924	Paris, France
IX	1928	Amsterdam, The Netherlands
X	1932	Los Angeles, U.S.A.
XI	1936	Berlin, Germany
XII	1940	Canceled due to WWII
XIII	1944	Canceled due to WWII
XIV	1948	London, England
XV	1952	Helsinki, Finland
XVI	1956	Melbourne, Australia
XVII	1960	Rome, Italy
XVIII	1964	Tokyo, Japan
XIX	1968	Mexico City, Mexico
XX	1972	Munich, Germany
XXI	1976	Montreal, Canada
XXII	1980	Moscow, USSR
XXIII	1984	Los Angeles, U.S.A.
XXIV	1988	Seoul, South Korea
XXV	1992	Barcelona, Spain
XXVI	1996	Atlanta, U.S.A.
XXVII	2000	Sydney, Australia
XXVIII	2004	Athens, Greece

The Olympic Winter Games

I	1924	Chamonix, France
II	1928	St. Moritz, Switzerland
III	1932	Lake Placid, U.S.A.
IV	1936	Garmisch-Partenkirchen, Germany
	1940	Canceled due to WWII
	1944	Canceled due to WWII
V	1948	St. Moritz, Switzerland
VI	1952	Oslo, Norway
VII	1956	Cortina D'Ampezzo, Italy
VIII	1960	Squaw Valley, U.S.A.
IX	1964	Innsbruck, Austria
X	1968	Grenoble, France
XI	1972	Sapporo, Japan
XII	1976	Innsbruck, Austria
XIII	1980	Lake Placid, U.S.A.
XIV	1984	Sarajevo, Yugoslavia
XV	1988	Calgary, Canada
XVI	1992	Albertville, France
XVII	1994	Lillehammer, Norway
XVIII	1998	Nagano, Japan
XIX	2002	Salt Lake City, U.S.A.
XX	2006	Turin, Italy

245. FACTS ABOUT THE SPECIAL OLYMPICS

➡ The Special Olympics is an international program of year-round sports training and athletic competition for more than one million children and adults with mental retardation.

➡ The Special Olympics oath is, "Let me win. But if I cannot win, let me be brave in the attempt."

➡ The benefits of participation in Special Olympics for people with mental retardation include improved physical fitness and motor skills, greater self-confidence, a more positive self-image, friendships, and increased family support.

➡ The Special Olympics began in 1968 when Eunice Kennedy Shriver organized the First International Special Olympics Games at Soldier Field in Chicago, Illinois.

➡ To be eligible to participate in the Special Olympics, a participant must be at least eight years old and identified by an agency or professional as having one of the following conditions: mental retardation, cognitive delays as measured by formal assessment, or significant learning or vocational problems due to cognitive delay that require or have required specially-designed instruction.

➡ More than 15,000 games, meets, and tournaments in both summer and winter sports are held worldwide each year.

➡ The Special Olympics provide year-round training and competition in 24 official sports:

Alpine Skiing	Bowling
Football (Soccer)	Sailing
Aquatics	Cycling
Golf	Softball
Athletics (Track and Field)	Equestrian
Gymnastics	Speed Skating
Badminton	Figure Skating
Nordic Skiing (Cross-Country)	Table Tennis
Basketball	Floor Hockey
Powerlifting	Team Handball
Bocce	Tennis
Roller Skating	Volleyball

246. TOURNAMENT DESIGN CONSIDERATIONS

➡ Objectives of the Tournament
- Determining a champion quickly?
- Providing maximum participation?
- Encouraging social interaction?
- Emphasizing competition?
- Providing equal participation?
- Developing skill?

➡ Characteristics of the Participants
- Age?
- Skill level?
- Interest and desire?
- Competitive or noncompetitive?

➡ Available Facilities and Equipment
- Number of available fields or courts?
- Amount of available equipment?
- Type of available equipment?

➡ Time Parameters
- Length of time?
- Specific dates?
- Weather dates?

➡ Type of Event

247. TYPES OF TOURNAMENTS

1. Round-Robin Tournament

➡ A round-robin tournament is run somewhat like a sports league.

➡ All of the teams are placed into divisions and must play a set number of games, usually playing every other team in their division.

➡ When this set number of games has been played, the top team(s) in each division move on to the second round, while all of the other teams are out of the tournament.

➡ In the second round, each team plays against every other remaining team.

➡ The team with the best record at the end of this round is the champion.

➡ If two teams end up tied for first, whoever wins the head-to-head game is the champion.

➡ Advantages:

- Easy to organize and understand
- Participants know in advance when they play
- Win–loss records don't matter
- Maximizes participation
- Produces a true champion
- Effective for outdoor programming
- Works well with smaller leagues

➡ Disadvantages:

- Time consuming
- Requires a great deal of facility use
- Forfeits occur more frequently in the last rounds
- Possible to end in a tie
- Does not produce an instant winner

➡ Formula for an Odd Number of Teams

- Assign a number to each team.
- Use those numbers when drawing up the schedule.
- For example, in a league with 7 teams, put the teams in the following order:

7	6	5	4	3	2	1
6-1	5-7	4-6	3-5	2-4	1-3	7-2
5-2	4-1	3-7	2-6	1-5	7-4	6-3
4-3	3-2	2-1	1-7	7-6	6-5	5-4

- The numbers go down on the right side and up on the left.
- All numbers revolve with one team drawing a bye.

➡ Formula for an Even Number of Teams

- Assign a number to each team.
- Use those numbers when drawing up the schedule.
- For example, in a league with 8 teams, put the teams in the following order:

1-2	1-8	1-7	1-6	1-5	1-4	1-3
8-3	7-2	6-8	5-7	4-6	3-5	2-4
7-4	6-3	5-2	4-8	3-7	2-6	8-5
6-5	5-4	4-3	3-2	2-8	8-7	7-6

- The number 1 position remains stationary.
- The other numbers revolve around number 1 until the original combination is again reached.

2. Bracket Tournaments

➡ A chart consisting of various brackets is designed in a bracketed tournament.

➡ Each bracket consists of eight teams.

➡ Every team in the tournament is placed on this chart.

➡ Teams play head-to-head against another team, with the winner moving on to the next round, while the loser is either out of the tournament (single-elimination) or is placed in the loser's bracket.

➡ When planning a bracketed tournament, the ideal number of teams is 8, 16, 32, or 64.

➡ If the ideal number of teams is not possible, some teams will get "bye" games and not have to play in the first round.

SINGLE-ELIMINATION BRACKET TOURNAMENT

➡ Advantages:

- Easy to understand
- Simple tournament to conduct
- Useful in determining a champion in a short period of time
- Appropriate for 1-day format
- Can be conducted with limited facilities
- Accommodates large numbers
- Interesting for spectators
- Efficient and economical

➡ Disadvantages:

- Minimum participation
- Emphasis is on winning
- Champions may not represent the best teams
- Does not allow for an "off-day"
- Competition can become intense
- Outdoor sports programs cause scheduling problems because contests must be played sequentially
- Provides least flexibility for participant

➡ Formula and Procedure:

- If participants are of equal or unknown strength, draw for positions in the bracket.
- If the strength of the participants is known, seed the best teams so that they do not meet in the early rounds.
- Place the seeded positions in the first, fifth, ninth, thirteenth, etc., positions.
- All byes must occur in the first round of play.
- The total number of games played is always one less than the number of entries.

- To determine the number of games the winner would have to play, count the powers of two in the number of entries. For example, with 32 entries, the winner will play 5 games (2 to the fifth power equals 32).

DOUBLE-ELIMINATION BRACKET TOURNAMENT

➡ Advantages:

- Fairest tournament

- Provides twice the participation

- Holds participant interest for a longer period of time

- Affords an entry an off-day

➡ Disadvantages:

- Confusing to participants

- Complicated to show graphically

- More time consuming

➡ Formula and Procedure:

- Two defeats eliminate an entry.

- The losers in the first rounds move into the loser's bracket.

- The teams that advance the farthest in both brackets meet each other in the final game.

- If the winner of the loser's bracket defeats the winner of the first-round bracket, the teams are rematched for the championship in order for one of the teams to have lost two games.

- Byes are assigned in the first round of the original elimination brackets.

- In the first round of the loser's bracket, byes must be arranged to avoid giving a second bye to any entry.

- In the loser's bracket, efforts must be made to avoid pairing entries that have met in earlier rounds.

© 2001 Parker Publishing Company

CONSOLATION TOURNAMENT

➝ Advantages:

- Good for providing entries with more than one game when there is not enough time to run a double elimination.

- More participation is provided than single elimination.

- Each entry is guaranteed at least two contests.

➝ Disadvantages:

- Not nearly so popular as single or double elimination because the loser can never come out of the bottom bracket and win the championship.

- Interest is sometimes lost if there is no chance for winning the championship.

- Forfeits are higher than in single-elimination tournaments.

➝ Type A: All losers in first round play in another single-elimination tournament (simple consolation).

➝ Type B: The loser out of any round drops down into consolation bracket (second-place consolation).

3. Challenge Tournament (Ladder Tournament)

➝ The competition is arranged by challenge and requires a minimum of supervision.

➝ A player may challenge either of the two players above him or her in the ladder.

➝ If the challenger wins, he or she exchanges places with the losing player in the ladder.

➝ All challenges must be accepted.

➝ Players draw for position in the ladder.

➝ Advantages:

- Easy to organize

- Requires minimum supervision

- Maximum participation; does not eliminate

- Winning not required for continued participation

- Affords opportunities for social interaction

- Participants play at their own convenience

- Good for skill development and practice

➝ Disadvantages:

- Communication can be difficult

- Lack of challenges for some participants

- Best suited to smaller numbers

- Can be complicated

➥ Procedure:

- All challenges must be accepted and played within a specific period of time.

- Predetermine challenge options:

    One level above only

    One or two levels above

    Any participant in the tournament

- Establish whose responsibility it is to update the board. (Typically the winner's responsibility.)

- Establish a minimum and maximum number of contests that may be played.

- Announce a definite date for the completion of the tournament.

- A final ranking of all players at end of tournament determines the winner.

248. BRACKET TOURNAMENT DIAGRAMS

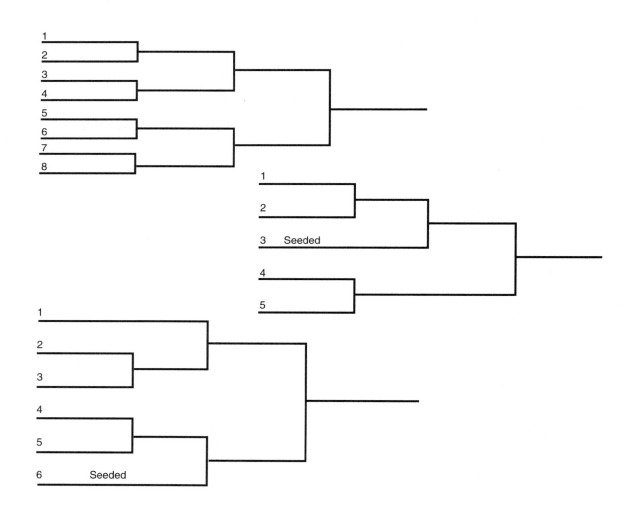

249. ROUND-ROBIN TOURNAMENT ROTATION SCHEDULES

Field or Court	**4-Team Schedule**		
A	2-1	4-2	4-1
B	3-4	1-3	2-3

Field or Court	**5-Team Schedule**				
A	1-4	3-1	5-3	2-5	4-2
B	2-3	4-5	1-2	3-4	5-1

Field or Court	**6-Team Schedule**				
A	2-1	3-4	6-4	5-3	5-6
B	4-5	6-1	2-3	6-2	1-3
C	3-6	2-5	1-5	4-1	4-2

Field or Court	**7-Team Schedule**						
A	1-6	4-2	2-7	5-3	3-1	6-4	7-5
B	2-5	5-1	3-6	6-2	4-7	7-3	1-4
C	3-4	6-7	4-5	7-1	5-6	1-2	2-3

Field or Court	**8-Team Schedule**						
A	5-6	3-4	7-8	7-5	1-3	3-6	8-2
B	3-8	1-7	6-2	6-1	4-2	4-5	7-3
C	4-7	8-6	4-1	2-3	5-8	2-7	1-5
D	2-1	2-5	5-3	8-4	6-7	8-1	3-4

Field or Court	**9-Team Schedule**							
A	1-8	5-3	2-9	6-4	3-1	7-5	4-2	8-6	9-7
B	2-7	6-2	3-8	7-3	4-9	8-4	5-1	9-5	1-6
C	3-6	7-1	4-7	8-2	5-8	9-3	6-9	1-4	2-5
D	4-5	8-9	5-6	9-1	6-7	1-2	7-8	2-3	3-4

Field or Court	**10-Team Schedule**							
A	2-1	10-4	6-9	10-6	5-3	1-9	7-3	5-6	8-4
B	5-8	1-7	7-8	2-5	6-2	10-8	6-4	1-10	9-3
C	4-9	8-6	3-1	3-4	7-10	2-7	5-1	2-9	6-1
D	3-10	9-5	4-2	1-8	8-9	3-6	8-2	4-7	7-5
E	6-7	2-3	5-10	9-7	4-1	4-5	9-10	3-8	10-2

Field or Court	**11-Team Schedule**									
A	1-10	6-4	2-11	7-5	3-1	8-6	4-2	9-7	5-3	10-8	11-9
B	2-9	7-3	3-10	8-4	4-11	9-5	5-1	10-6	6-2	11-7	1-8
C	3-8	8-2	4-9	9-3	5-10	10-4	6-11	11-5	7-1	1-6	2-7
D	4-7	9-1	5-8	10-2	6-9	11-3	7-10	1-4	8-11	2-5	3-6
E	5-6	10-11	6-7	11-1	7-8	1-2	8-9	2-3	9-10	3-4	4-5

Field or Court	**12-Team Schedule**									
A	6-9	11-3	5-8	10-11	12-8	4-2	8-1	9-3	4-7	7-12	1-9
B	3-12	10-4	2-11	9-12	4-5	5-12	9-7	6-1	3-8	6-2	10-8
C	4-11	8-6	12-1	8-2	3-6	7-10	10-6	7-5	1-11	9-10	2-5
D	5-10	9-5	6-7	1-5	2-7	6-11	2-3	8-4	12-10	4-1	3-4
E	2-1	1-7	3-10	6-4	10-1	8-9	12-4	11-12	2-9	5-3	11-7
F	7-8	12-2	4-9	7-3	11-9	1-3	11-5	10-2	5-6	8-11	12-6

250. PHYSICAL EDUCATION QUOTATIONS

Winning is not a sometime thing; it's an all time thing. You don't win once in a while, you don't do things right once in a while, you do them right all the time. Winning is habit. Unfortunately, so is losing.

—*Vince Lombardi*

You have to expect things of yourself before you can do them.

—*Michael Jordan*

Do not let what you cannot do interfere with what you can do.

—*John Wooden*

If you train hard, you'll not only be hard, you'll be hard to beat.

—*Herschel Walker*

Most games are lost, not won.

—*Casey Stengel*

The minute you start talking about what you're going to do if you lose, you have lost.

—*George Shultz*

Adversity causes some men to break; others to break records.

—*William A. Ward*

Sweat plus sacrifice equals success.

—*Charlie Finley*

You have no control over what the other guy does. You only have control over what you do.

—*A J Kitt*

It's not the size of the dog in the fight, but the size of the fight in the dog.

—*Archie Griffen, 5'9" two-time Heisman winner*

There's no substitute for guts.

—*Paul "Bear" Bryant*

How you respond to the challenge in the second half will determine what you become after the game, whether you are a winner or a loser.

—*Lou Holtz*

My motto was always to keep swinging. Whether I was in a slump or feeling badly or having trouble off the field, the only thing to do was keep swinging.

—*Hank Aaron*

Besides pride, loyalty, discipline, heart, and mind, confidence is the key to all the locks.

—Joe Paterno

The will to win is important, but the will to prepare is vital.

—Joe Paterno

It's lack of faith that makes people afraid of meeting challenges, and I believed in myself.

—Muhammad Ali

Power is not revealed by striking hard or often, but by striking true.

—Honoré de Balzac

To succeed . . . You need to find something to hold on to, something to motivate you, something to inspire you.

—Tony Dorsett

Ask not what your teammates can do for you. Ask what you can do for your teammates.

—Magic Johnson

Set your goals high, and don't stop till you get there.

—Bo Jackson

Nobody climbs mountains for scientific reasons. Science is used to raise money for the expeditions, but you really climb for the hell of it.

—Sir Edmund Hillary

I learned that if you want to make it bad enough, no matter how bad it is, you can make it.

—Gale Sayers

The difference between the impossible and the possible lies in a man's determination.

—Tommy Lasorda

Luck is what happens when preparation meets opportunity.

—Darrel Royal

You can become a winner only if you are willing to walk over the edge.

—Damon Runyon

It's a little like wrestling a gorilla. You don't quit when you're tired—you quit when the gorilla is tired.

—Robert Strauss

If you can believe it, the mind can achieve it.

—Ronnie Lott

The mind is the limit. As long as the mind can envision the fact that you can do something, you can do it—as long as you really believe 100 percent.

—Arnold Schwarzenegger

Setting a goal is not the main thing. It is deciding how you will go about achieving it and staying with that plan.

—Tom Landry

Winners never quit and quitters never win.

—Anonymous

It's not necessarily the amount of time you spend at practice that counts; it's what you put into the practice.

—Eric Lindros

The only place where success comes before work is in the dictionary.

—Vidal Sassoon

The best and fastest way to learn a sport is to watch and imitate a champion.

—Jean-Claude Killy

Courage is resistance to fear, mastery of fear—not absence of fear.

—Mark Twain

Show me a guy who's afraid to look bad, and I'll show you a guy you can beat every time.

—Lou Brock

Don't look back. Something might be gaining on you.

—Satchel Paige

If at first you don't succeed, you are running about average.

—M. H. Alderson

When someone tells me there is only one way to do things, it always lights a fire under my butt. My instant reaction is, "I'm gonna prove you wrong."

—Picabo Street

The price of success is hard work, dedication to the job at hand, and the determination that whether we win or lose, we have applied the best of ourselves to the task at hand.

—Vince Lombardi

There are only two options regarding commitment. You're either IN or you're OUT. There's no such thing as life in-between.

—Pat Riley

The game isn't over till it's over.

—*Yogi Berra*

It's what you learn after you know it all that counts.

—*John Wooden*

I'm a great believer in luck, and I find the harder I work, the more I have of it.

—*Thomas Jefferson*

When you're riding, only the race in which you're riding is important.

—*Bill Shoemaker*

It is a rough road that leads to the heights of greatness.

—*Seneca*

The way a team plays as a whole determines its success. You may have the greatest bunch of individual stars in the world, but if they don't play together, the club won't be worth a dime.

—*Babe Ruth*

The day you take complete responsibility for yourself, the day you stop making any excuses, that's the day you start to the top.

—*O. J. Simpson*

Before you can win a game, you have to not lose it.

—*Chuck Noll*

The difference between a successful person and others is not a lack of strength, not a lack of knowledge, but rather a lack of will.

—*Vince Lombardi*

Only those who dare to fail greatly can ever achieve greatly.

—*Robert F. Kennedy*

My thoughts before a big race are usually pretty simple. I tell myself: "Get out of the blocks, run your race, stay relaxed. If you run your race, you'll win. . . . Channel your energy. Focus."

—*Carl Lewis*

The winners in life think constantly in terms of I can, I will, and I am. Losers, on the other hand, concentrate their waking thoughts on what they should have or would have done, or what they can't do.

—*Dennis Waitley*

Genius is one percent inspiration and ninety-nine percent perspiration.

—*Thomas Edison*

A ship in the harbor is safe. But that's not what ships are built for.

—*Anonymous*

The best inspiration is not to outdo others, but to outdo ourselves.

—*Anonymous*

Think big, believe big, act big, and the results will be big.

—*Anonymous*

Nothing in the world can take the place of persistence. Talent will not: Nothing is more common than unsuccessful men with talent. Genius will not: Unrewarded genius is almost a proverb. Education will not: The world is full of educated derelicts. Persistence and determination alone are omnipotent.

—*Anonymous*

You learn you can do your best even when it's hard, even when you're tired and maybe hurting a little bit. It feels good to show some courage.

—*Joe Namath*

Winning isn't everything, wanting to is.

—*Anonymous*

If you don't do what's best for your body, you're the one who comes up on the short end.

—*Julius Erving*

Confidence is a very fragile thing.

—*Joe Montana*

If you set a goal for yourself and are able to achieve it, you have won your race. Your goal can be to come in first, to improve your performance, or just finish the race—it's up to you.

—*Dave Scott*

I've always made a total effort, even when the odds seemed entirely against me. I never quit trying; I never felt that I didn't have a chance to win.

—*Arnold Palmer*

Physical fitness is not only one of the most important keys to a healthy body, it is the basis of dynamic and creative intellectual activity. The relationship between the soundness of the body and the activities of the mind is subtle and complex. Much is not yet understood. But we do know what the Greeks knew: that intelligence and skill can only function at the peak of their capacity when the body is healthy and strong; that hardy spirits and tough minds usually inhabit sound gods.

—*John F. Kennedy*

The world is full of willing people, some willing to work, the others willing to let them.

—*Robert Frost*

The more I train, the more I realize I have more speed in me.

—*Leroy Burrell*

Each Warrior wants to leave the mark of his will, his signature, on important acts he touches. This is not the voice of ego but of the human spirit, rising up and declaring that it has something to contribute to the solution of the hardest problems, no matter how vexing!

—*Pat Riley*

If you chase two rabbits, both will escape.

—*Anonymous*

Even if you are on the right track, you'll get run over if you just sit there.

—*Will Rogers*

Winners never quit and quitters never win.

—*Anonymous*

I will always be someone who wants to do better than others. I love competition.

—*Jean-Claude Killy*

Great works are performed not by strength but by perseverance.

—*Samuel Johnson*

Other people may not have had high expectations for me . . . but I had high expectations for myself.

—*Shannon Miller*

I always felt that my greatest asset was not my physical ability, it was my mental ability.

—*Bruce Jenner*

In order to win you must be prepared to lose sometime. And leave one or two cards showing.

—*Van Morrison*

He who stops being better stops being good.

—*Oliver Cromwell*

The principle is competing against yourself. It's about self-improvement, about being better than you were the day before.

—*Steve Young*

When elephants fight, it is the grass that suffers.

—*Kikuyu proverb*

I know that I'm never as good or bad as any single performance. I've never believed my critics or my worshippers, and I've always been able to leave the game at the arena.

—*Charles Barkley*

A winner never whines.

—Paul Brown

What's the worst thing that can happen to a quarterback? He loses his confidence.

—Terry Bradshaw

Ain't no chance if you don't take it.

—Guy Clark

In war there is no substitute for victory.

—Douglas MacArthur

You do not merely want to be considered just the best of the best. You want to be considered the only ones who do what you do.

—Jerry Garcia, The Grateful Dead

The first and great commandment is, Don't let them scare you.

—Elmer Davis

I think I've always had the shots. But in the past, I've suffered too many mental lapses. Now, I'm starting to get away from that and my mental discipline and commitment to the game are much better. I think I'm really taking a good look at the big picture. That's the difference between being around for the final or watching the final from my sofa at home.

—Andre Agassi

When you face a fork in the road, step on the exhilarator!

—Pat Riley

You need to play with supreme confidence, or else you'll lose again, and then losing becomes a habit.

—Joe Paterno

You have to perform at a consistently higher level than others. That's the mark of a true professional.

—Joe Paterno

Concentration is the ability to think about absolutely nothing when it is absolutely necessary.

—Ray Knight

To be prepared is half the victory.

—Miguel Cervantes

251. WAYS TO PRAISE

A+ job

A+ work

Amazing effort!

Awesome

Beautiful

Beautiful sharing

Beautiful work

Bingo

Bravo

Breathtaking!

Congratulations!

Cool!

Creative job

Creative work

Dynamite

Exactly right

Excellent!

Exceptional!

Exceptional performance

Fabulous!

Fantastic

Fantastic job

Fantastic work

Far out!

Good

Good attempt

Good for you

Good job

Good stuff

Good thinking

Good work

Great

Great answer

Great discovery

Hip, hip, hooray

Hooray for you

Hot dog

Hot stuff

How artistic

How did you do that?

How does that make you feel?

How extraordinary!

How nice

How original

How smart

How thoughtful of you

I appreciate what you've done

I believe you'll handle it

I can see progress

I can tell you really care

I can't get over it!

I couldn't have done it better

I have confidence in your judgment

I knew you could do it

I knew you had it in you!

I like the way you handled that

I like the way you worked that out

I like the way you . . .

I like the way you're working

I like you

I like your work

I respect you

I think the others would like to see

I trust you

I'm glad you're here

I'm proud of you

It couldn't be better!

It looks like you put a lot of work into this

It makes me happy when people work together

It must make you feel good that . . .

It's everything that I hoped for!

It's fun to play on your team

Keep up the good work

Let's try again

Look how far you've come

Looking good

Magnificent

Marvelous

Much better

Neat

Nice going

Nice try

Nice work

No one says it quite like you

Not bad

Nothing can stop you now

Now you have it

Now you're flying

Now you've got it

Now you've got the hang of it

Oh, I see your point

Outstanding

Outstanding performance

Perfect

Phenomenal!

Radical

Remarkable

Remarkable job

Right on!

Sensational!

Spectacular

Spectacular job

Spectacular work

Super

Super job

Super work

Superb!

Superstar

Take a bow

Terrific

Terrific effort!

Thank you

Thank you very much

Thanks for being honest

Thanks for caring

Thanks for helping

Thanks for sharing

Thanks for trying

That was first-class work

That's a good point

That's a very good observation

That's an interesting point

That's an interesting way of looking at it

That's better than ever

That's clever

That's coming along nicely

That's correct

That's encouraging

That's going to be great

That's good

That's great

That's hot

That's incredible

That's it

That's much better

That's quite an improvement

That's really nice

That's right

That's the best

That's the way to do it

That's the way to handle it

The time you put in really shows!

Thumbs up

Try your best

Unbelievable work

Very brave

Very creative

Very good

Very impressive

Way to be on task

Way to go

Well done

What a genius!

What a good listener

What a great idea

What an imagination!

What neat work!

Wonderful!

Wow!

You are doing a good job

You are exciting

You are fun

You are responsible

You are so helpful

You are very good at that

You belong

You brighten my day

You came through!

You can be trusted

You can do it

You care

You did a lot of work today

You did that very well

You figured it out!

You figured that out fast

You just about have it

You learned it right

You made it happen!

You made my day

You made the difference

You make it look easy

You make me happy

You make me laugh

You mean a lot to me

You must have been practicing

You outdid yourself today

You really outdid yourself

You really paid attention!

You really tried

You should be proud of yourself!

You tried hard

You'll make it

You're getting there

Your help counts!

Your project is first-rate

Your work is out of sight

You're #1

You're a big help

You're a champ

You're a good friend

You're a good friend because you . . .

You're a good leader

You're a great example for others!

You're a great kid

You're a joy

You're a pleasure to know

You're a real trooper

You're a shining star

You're a treasure

You're amazing

You're a-okay

You're beautiful

You're catching on

You're darling

You're doing a lot better

You're doing so well

You're fantastic

You're getting better

You're growing up

You're important

You're improving

You're incredible

You're making progress

You're neat

You're on it

You're on target

You're on the right track now

You're on top of it

You're on your way

You're perfect

You're right on track

You're really working hard today

You're sensational

You're sharp

You're so kind

You're so smart

You're special

You're super!

You're the best

You're the greatest

You're tops

You're unique

You're very talented

You're wonderful

You've discovered the secret

You've earned my respect

You've got it now

You've got it right

You've got it!

You've got what it takes

You've got your brain in gear

You've made progress

You've outdone yourself!

You've really grown up

252. MULTISPORT ORGANIZATIONS

Organization	Address/Phone	Website
Amateur Athletic Association	1-800-AAU-4USA	www.aausports.org/
American Alliance for Health, Physical Education, Recreation and Dance	1900 Association Drive Reston, VA 20191 (703) 476-3400; (800) 213-7193	www.aahperd.org/
American Council on Exercise	5820 Oberlin Drive, Suite 102 San Diego, CA 92121-3787 (858) 535-8227; Fax: (858) 535-1778	www.acefitness.org/
National Alliance for Youth Sports	2050 Vista Parkway West Palm Beach, FL 33411 (561) 684-1141; Fax: (561) 684-2546 (800) 729-2057; (800) 688-KIDS	www.nays.org
National Association of Police Athletic Leagues (PAL)	General Manager 618 North U.S. Highway 1, Suite 201 North Palm Beach, FL 33408-5696 (407) 844-1823; Fax: (407) 863-6120	
National Collegiate Athletic Association	700 W. Washington Avenue P.O. Box 6222 Indianapolis, IN 46206-6222 (317) 917-6222; (317) 917-6888	www.ncaa.org
National Federation of State High School Associations	P.O. Box 690 Indianapolis, IN 46206 (317) 972-6900; Fax: (317) 822-5700	www.nfhs.org
National Intramural–Recreational Sports Association	4185 SW Research Way Corvallis, OR 97333-1067 (541) 766-8211; Fax: (541) 766-8284	www.nirsa.org
President's Council on Physical Fitness and Sports	200 Independence Avenue SW Suite 738-H Washington, DC 20201 (202) 690-9000; Fax: (202) 690-5211	www.surgeongeneral.gov
United States Olympic Committee		www.usoc.org
YMCA of the USA	101 North Wacker Drive Chicago, IL 60606 (312) 977-0031	www.ymca.net
YWCA of the USA	Empire State Building 350 Fifth Avenue, Suite 301 New York, NY 10118 (212) 273-7800; Fax: (212) 465-2281	www.ywca.org

253. SPECIAL SPORT ORGANIZATIONS

Organization	Address/Phone	Website
Amputee Coalition of America	900 E. Hill Avenue, Suite 285 Knoxville, TN 37915-2568 (888) AMP-KNOW	www.amuptee-coalition.org
Disabled Sports USA	451 Hungerford Drive, Suite 100 Rockville, MD 20850 (301) 217-0960	www.dsusa.org
Dwarf Athletic Association of America	418 Willow Way Lewisville, TX 75067 (972) 317-8299	www.daaa.org
Paralyzed Veterans of America (National)	900 17th Street NW, Suite 400 Washington DC 20006 (800) 424-8200	www.pva.org
The International Paralympic Committee	USOC Disabled Services One Olympic Plaza Colorado Springs, CO 80909 (719) 578-4818	www.paralympic.org
United Amputee Services Association	P.O. Box 4277 Winter Park, FL 32793-4277 (407) 678-2920	www.oandp.com
United States Association of Blind Athletes	33 North Institute Street Colorado Springs, CO 80903 (719) 630-0422	www.usaba.org
United States Cerebral Palsy Athletic Association	200 Harrison Avenue Newport, RI 02840 (401) 848-2460	www.uscpaa.org
Wheelchair Athletics of the USA	2351 Parkwood Road Snellville, GA 30278 (770) 972-0763	
Wheelchair Sports USA	3595 E. Fountain Boulevard, Suite L-1 Colorado Springs, CO 80910 (719) 574-1150	www.wsusa.org
World T.E.A.M. (The Exceptional Athlete Matters) Sports	2108 South Boulevard, Suite 101 Charlotte, NC 28203 (704) 370-6070	www.worldteamsports.org

254. SPORT-SPECIFIC ORGANIZATIONS

Sport	Organization/Address/Phone	Website
Archery	National Archery Association One Olympic Plaza Colorado Springs, CO 80909 (719) 578-4576; Fax: (719) 632-4733	www.usarchery.org
Badminton	USA Badminton One Olympic Plaza Colorado Springs, CO 80909 (719) 578-4808; Fax: (719) 578-4507	www.usabadminton.org
Basketball	USA Basketball Publications 5465 Mark Dabling Boulevard Colorado Springs, CO 80918	www.usabasketball.com
Bocce	World Bocce Association 1098 W. Irving Park Road Bensenville, IL 60106 (630) 860-BOCE; Fax: (630) 595-2541	www.worldbocce.org/USA/
Bowling	Bowling Headquarters 5301 South 76th Street Greendale, WI 53129 (414) 421-9000	www.usabowling.org/
Fencing	United States Fencing Association One Olympic Plaza Colorado Springs, CO 80909 (719) 578-4511; Fax: (719) 632-5737	www.usfa.org/
Field Hockey	United States Field Hockey Association One Olympic Plaza Colorado Springs, CO 80909 (719) 578-4567; Fax: (719) 632-0979	www.usfieldhockey.com/usfha/
Fitness	National Strength and Conditioning Association 1955 N. Union Boulevard Colorado Springs, CO 80909 (719) 632-6722; (800) 815-6826 Fax: (719) 632-6367	www.nsca-lift.org/

Sport	Organization/Address/Phone	Website
Flag Football	American Football Association P.O. Box 43885 Las Vegas, NV 89116	www.afafootball.com/
Frisbee™	Ultimate Players Association 3595 E. Fountain Boulevard, Suite J2 Colorado Springs, CO 80910	www.upa.org
	Freestyle Players Association P.O. Box 2612 Del Mar, CA 92014-2612	www.freestyledisc.org/
Golf	The United States Golf Association P.O. Box 708 Far Hills, NJ 07931 (908) 234-2300; Fax: (908) 234-9687	www.usga.org/
Gymnastics	USA Gymnastics Pan American Plaza 201 S. Capitol Ave., Suite 300 Indianapolis, IN 46225 (317) 237-5050; Fax: (317) 237-5069	www.usa-gymnastics.org/
Handball	USA Team Handball 1903 Powers Ferry Road, Suite 230 Atlanta, GA 30339 (770) 956-7660; (888) Play-THB Fax: (770) 956-7976	www.usateamhandball.org/
Horseshoes	NHPA 3085 76th Street Franksville, WI 53126 Phone/Fax: (262) 835-9108	www.horseshoepitching.com/
Juggling	International Jugglers Association Braidy Brown, Board Chairman 1197 Cornell Avenue Binghamton, NY 13901 (607) 724-0538	www.juggle.org/
Jump Rope	USAJRF P.O. Box 569 Huntsville, TX 77342 (936) 295-3332; (800) 225-8820 Fax: (936) 295-3309	www.usajrf.org/

Sport	Organization/Address/Phone	Website
	USAJRF Headquarters 1523 Normal Park, Suite G Huntsville, TX 77340	www.usajrf.org/
Lacrosse	US Lacrosse 113 W. University Parkway Baltimore, MD 21210 (410) 235-6882 Fax: (410) 366-6735	www.lacrosse.org/
Pickleball	USAPA 3504 Fox Spit Road Langley, WA 98260 (888) 775-9615	www.usapa.org/
Soccer	United States Youth Soccer Association 899 Presidential Drive, Suite 117 Richardson, TX 75081 (800) 4SOCCER	www.usysa.org
	United States Soccer Federation 1801–1811 South Prairie Avenue Chicago, IL 60616	www.us-soccer.com/
Table Tennis	USA Table Tennis One Olympic Plaza Colorado Springs, CO 80909 (719) 578-4583; Fax: (719) 632-6071	www.usatt.org
Tennis	U.S. Tennis Association P.O. Box 5046 White Plains, NY 10602 (800) 990-USTA (8782)	www.usta.com
Track and Field	USA Track & Field One RCA Dome, Suite 140 Postal: P.O. Box 120 Indianapolis, IN 46225	www.usatf.org/
Volleyball	United States Youth Volleyball League 12501 South Isis Avenue Hawthorne, CA 90250 (310) 643-8398; (888) 988-7985 Fax: (310) 643-8396	www.volleyball.org/usyvl/

Sport	Organization/Address/Phone	Website
	USA Volleyball 715 S. Circle Drive Colorado Springs, CO 80910 Voice: (719) 228-6800 Fax: (719) 228-6899 Information Line: (888) 786-5539	www.usatf.org/
Weight Training	USA Weightlifting One Olympic Plaza Colorado Springs, CO 80909 (719) 578-4508; Fax: (719) 578-4741	www.usaweightlifting.org/
Wrestling	USA Wrestling 6155 Lehman Drive Colorado Springs, CO 80918 Voice: (719) 598-8181 Fax: (719) 598-9440	www.usawrestling.org/

NOTES

NOTES

NOTES

NOTES